Arched Window Solutions

Arched Window Solutions

By
Diane Deeds (Patentee)

Copyright © 2000 by Diane Deeds
All rights reserved.
No part of this book may be reproduced, stored in a retrieval system, or transmitted by any means, electronic, mechanical, photocopying, recording or otherwise, without the written concent of the author.

ISBN# 1-58721-035-5

About the Book

You too can now have the look of designer drapes for arched windows, that previously could only be obtained by hiring an expensive Interior Decorator. Before now these Palladian arched drapes, with lavish amounts of luxurious heavy, rich fabrics could only be placed on costly custom designed boards. Now you can pile on tufts of fabric and trim for that custom made look for only a fraction of the cost of hiring a decorator.

By following the instructions in this book, you will have a drapery board that fits most arched windows, and can be installed with commonly used tools.

This simple book, with large easy to read at a working distance print, will give you step by step instructions along with graphic illustrations to make your own designer drapes, even if you don't own a sewing machine. In fact you can have an arched window treatment even if you don't have an arched window.

Dedications

This book is dedicated to family and friends. To Rita who helped me see the need to share my idea with the public, and to my sister Tina who helped with the editing.

Table of Contents

INTRODUCTION XI

WARNINGS AND SAFETY INSTRUCTIONS XII

WHAT YOU MUST KNOW ABOUT THE POYSTYRENE MOULDING MOUNTING BOARDS XIII

KNOW WHICH POLYSTYRENE MOULDING MOUNTING BOARD TO USE XIV

KNOW WHICH POLYSTYRENE MOULDING MOUNTING BOARD TO USE XV

GENERAL TOOLS NEEDED XVI

GENERAL SEWING SUPPLIES XVII

GENERAL SEWING SUPPLIES XVIII

GENERAL SEWING CONSIDERATIONS XIX

PREFACE XXI

WINDOW TREATMENTS AND THEIR CHAPTERS XXII

CHAPTER 1 THE OUTSIDE MOUNT 1

CHAPTER 2 OUTSIDE MOUNT FOR WINDOWS LARGER THAN 51" 19

CHAPTER 3   THE INSIDE MOUNT 37

CHAPTER 4   NO SEW GATHERED SHEET DRAPES WITH COVERED JUTE WEBBING OR A SIMPLY COVERED CRINOLINE 53

CHAPTER 5   ROD POCKET SLEEVE DRAPERY PANELS WITH A DIAGONAL CUT TO FIT ARCHED WINDOWS 91

CHAPTER 6   TWO SHORT SIDE BOARDS DRAPERY PANELS 113

CHAPTER 7   OUTSIDE MOUNT TRIPLE SWAG 131

CHAPTER 8   HALF DIMENSION SWAGS 169

CHAPTER 9   SINGLE SWAG 203

CHAPTER 10   SIMPLE NO SEW DRAPES WITH BRASS TIE BACKS 215

CHAPTER 11   PROPORTION CALCULATIONS TO MAKE SWAGS SIZES IN PROPORTION WHEN WINDOW SIZES VARY 239

CHAPTER 12   HOW TO GIVE A TRADITIONAL SQUARE WINDOW A PALLADIAN ARCHED LOOK 245

GLOSSARY 251

ABOUT THE AUTHOR 258

Introduction

If you will, imagine the stem of a flower. If you bend the stem back and forth it will break. If you bend the stem too fast or severely, it will break. But if you bend the stem slowly in a soft gentle curve allowing it to adjust to the new shape it will conform gracefully into an arch. The same is true for the Poystyrene Moulding Mounting Board. A slow gentle motion will allow it to adapt and mold itself into a soft curve, but if it is bent too fast, it is likely to snap and break. For this reason safety glasses must be worn at all times when handling the Polystyrene Moulding Mounting Board. See Warning and Safety Instructions regarding the handling of the Polystyrene Moulding Mounting Board.

If for any reason you wish to remove your Polystyrene Moulding Mounting Board, then purchase a new one rather than trying to remove and reuse the old one. This is because it will have molded somewhat to the arch's shape and will not tolerate a remolding. These Polystyrene Moulding Mounting Boards are fairly inexpensive.

WARNINGS AND SAFETY INSTRUCTIONS

The following safety instructions pertain particularly to the use and inherent properties of the possible breakage of the Polystyrene Moulding Mounting Board (abbreviated as P.M.M.Borard*):

(1) **SAFETY GLASSES SHOULD BE WORN AT ALL TIMES BY ALL PERSONS in the work area while handling the P.M.M. Board*.**

(2) **NEVER BALANCE YOURSELF WITH THE P.M.M. BOARD* as should it break you could lose your balance and fall. Always maintain your balance away from the P.M.M. Board*, never leaning on it.**

(3) **NEVER BEND A BARE P.M.M. Board* WITH METAL OBJECTS such as screws or thumbtacks in it, should it break these objects could become projectile. Always have fabric or tape covering the P.M.M. Board* to help catch these objects.**

(4) **The corner irons should always be securely fastened to the wall first and then gently bend the P.M.M. Board* to meet each corner iron and secure with screws. Never try to first put the corner irons in the P.M.M. Board* and then try to bend it in position to be secured to the wall.**

(5) **Do not put any additional holes in it or bend it back and forth before mounting.**

(6) **Do not use the P.M.M. Board* on windows with a width less than 36", or a height greater than 10'.**

(7) **Do not allow children or pets in the work area.**

What You Must Know About the Poystyrene Moulding Mounting Boards

The Poystyrene Moulding Mounting Boards are made of a strong flexible material that can hold the weight of today's heavy and luxurious designer fabrics with ease, but these wonderful boards do have their limits. The Polystyrene Moulding Mounting Board does not tolerate a back and forth motion which can weaken the integrity of it, nor can it fit a window smaller than 36". Also too many holes near the same area, bending it too fast or severely may cause it to break. Store them at room temperature as extreme cold may cause them to become brittle when attempting to bend them.

Over view of the Outside Mount of the Polystyrene Moulding Mounting Board

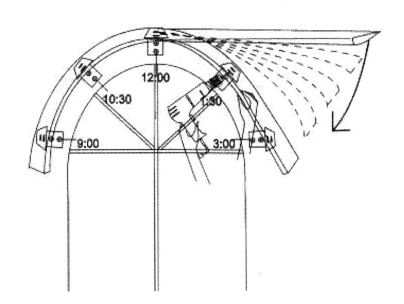

However, if the Polystyrene Moulding Mounting Board is handled gently during an outside mount, most people will find it quite easy with which to work. Safety glasses are required at all times during handling of the Polystyrene Moulding Mounting Board. Carefully read the WARNING AND SAFETY INSTRUCTIONS.

Know Which Polystyrene Moulding Mounting Board to Use

The Polystyrene Moulding Boards can be found in the Decorative Crown Moulding Center of your local hardware store. **"Marley Decorative Mouldings"** is the brand of polystyrene moulding boards used by the author of this book for this project. Only certain Polystyrene Moulding Boards are suitable for arched window treatments. Some Polystyrene boards at first glance may appear well suited, but in reality, they may have a much higher tendency for breakage as detailed below.

The Polystyrene Lattice Strip 5/32" x 1 1/8", which is flat, small, and thin is quite bendable and will tolerate a back and forth motion and a more extreme arching than the Polystyrene Moulding Mounting Board, but it does not have the strength to hold heavy weighted fabrics. The two are often used in combination to provide strength and flexibility. It may be used on windows with a width less than 36", by using smaller corner irons and lighter weighted fabrics.

The illustration below shows how plain, flat, thin, and small the dimensions of the **Polystyrene Lattice Strip** are.

Polystyrene Lattice Strip 5/32" x 1 1/8"

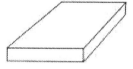

This makes it extremely suitable for bending. The thicker, wider, and curvier the Polystyrene Moulding Board gets, the less bendable it becomes.

Know Which Polystyrene Moulding Mounting Board to Use

The Colonial Base or Casing Polystyrene Moulding Board is much too curvy and thick to be suitable for bending and has a much higher tendency for breakage as shown in the illustration below.

Too curvy and thick for bending

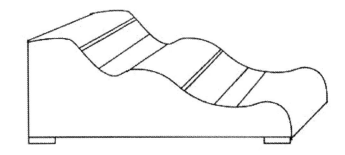

As illustrated below the **just right** Polystyrene Moulding Mounting Board is the **Ranch Base** 1/2" x 3 1/4".

Ranch Base 1/2" x 3 1/4"

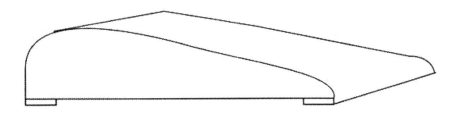

The Ranch Base 1 /2" x 2 7/ 16" may make a good substitute if the Ranch Base 1/2" x 3 1/4" is unavailable.

General Tools Needed

These are the general tools needed to mount the hardware. For the hardware and other materials needed, see each chapter's "Checklist For Tools and Supplies" page.

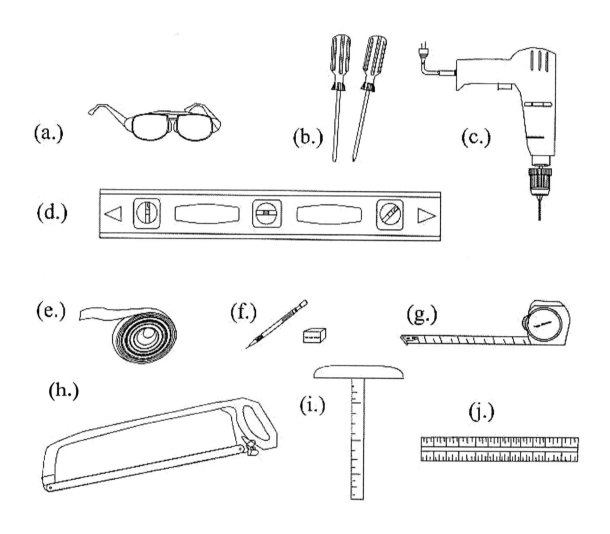

(a.) Safety glasses   (b.) Flat head and Phillips screwdriver
(c.) Electric drill   (d.) Level
(e.) Masking tape   (f.) Pencil and Art gum eraser
(g.) Tape measure   (h.) Hack saw (for chapter 6)
(i.) T-square   (j.) Ruler

General Sewing Supplies

These are the general sewing supplies needed for most of the window treatments, also continued on the following page. See each chapter's "Checklist For Tools and Supplies" page for particular supplies needed for that particular window treatment (sew or no sew).

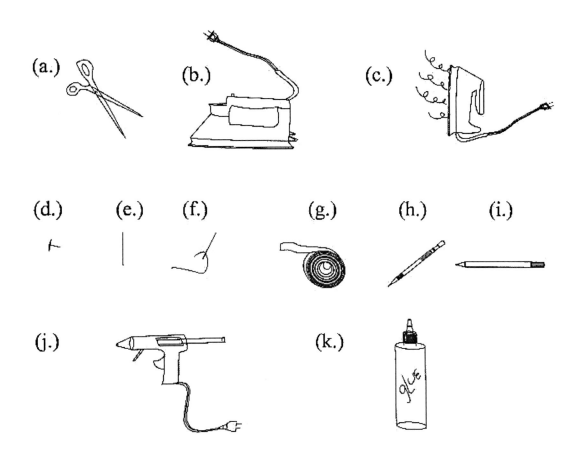

(a.) Scissors (b.) Iron
(c.) Travel steam Iron (d.) Thumbtack
(e.) Straight pin (f.) Needle
(g.) Masking tape (h.) Pencil
(i.) Disappearing ink pen (j.) Hot glue gun
(k.) Fabric glue

General Sewing Supplies

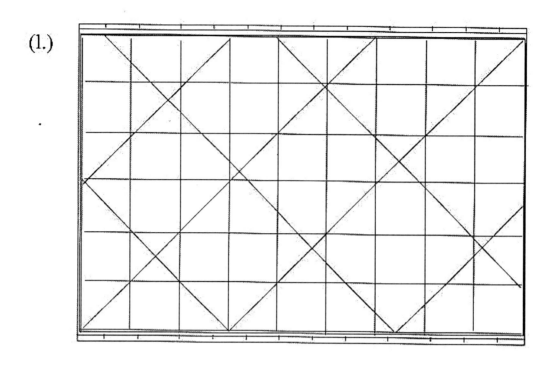

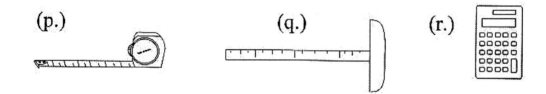

(l.) Fold up grid lined cutting board (m.) Sewing gauge
(n.) Ruler (o.) Yardstick
(p.) Tape measure (q.) T-square
(r.) Calculator

General Sewing Considerations

When purchasing fabric for a window treatment, try to buy it all at one time so it will be in the same dye lot. If placing an order, ask the fabric store sales person to assure it will be in the same dye lot.

Also consider that if purchasing fabric with a large decorative print, an extra repeat of fabric is needed for each drapery panel and swag so the whole window treatment will appear even and uniform. Measure and cut at the same point in the repeat of the print for each panel and swag.

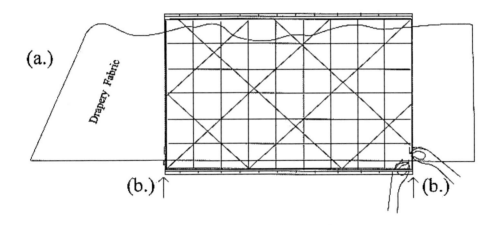

(a.) The fold up cardboard grid lined cutting board is fairly inexpensive and handy to have when measuring and cutting large amounts of fabric. It also takes the fear out of accidentally cutting, poking, or scratching, a table top, bedspread, or carpet by protecting these surfaces. Use either increments of measurement, inches or yards, which ever is most comfortable.

(b.) Place a pin at an easy to remember number at intervals so it will be easy to count what is needed and where to cut.

Preface

The first three chapters of this book show how to mount the hardware and the Polystyrene Moulding Mounting Board to the wall, or the inside window frame. The "Outside Mount" is a much easier mount than the "Inside Mount" as explained in their respective chapters.

Chapters 4 through 10 show the sew and no sew ways to make and apply the drapery fabric and lining to the arched Polystyrene Moulding Mounting Board. Browse to find the window treatment that best suits your window needs.

In this book, the top treatments are swags, "Outside Mount Triple Swags", "Single Swag", and "Half Dimensions Swags". These chapters will refer back to the under drapery treatment chapters, "Two Short Side Boards Drapery Panels", and "Rod Pocket Sleeve Drapery Panels with Diagonal Cut to Fit Arched Windows".

Chapters "No Sew Gathered Sheet Drapes", and "Simple No Sew Drapes with Brass Tie Backs" are very easy to do projects for even the most novice of beginners.

Chapters 11 and 12 show how to make swags sizes in proportion when window sizes vary, and how to give a palladian look to a traditional square window.

The following page illustrates the various different window treatments and their chapters.

Window Treatments and Their Chapters

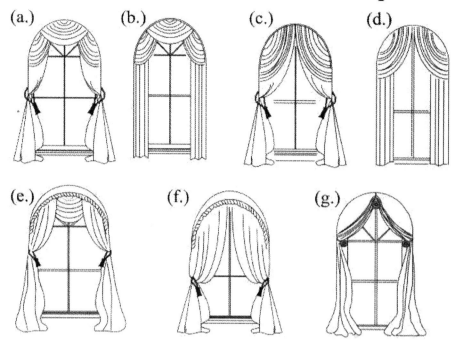

(a.) "Outside Mount Triple Swag" Chapter 7 with Chapter 5 drapery panel.

(b.) "Outside Mount Triple Swag" Chapter 7 with Chapter 6 drapery panel.

(c.) "Half Dimension Swags" Chapter 8 with Chapter 5 drapery panel.

(d.) "Half Dimension Swags" Chapter 8 with Chapter 6 drapery panel.

(e.) "Single Swag" Chapter 9 with Chapter 5 drapery panels.

(f.) "No Sew Gathered Sheet Drapes with Covered Jute Webbing or a Simply Covered Crinoline" Chapter 4.

(g.) "Simple No Sew Drapes with Brass Tie Backs" Chapter 10.

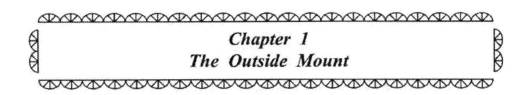

Chapter 1
The Outside Mount

This chapter deals with the mounting of the hardware and the P.M.M. Board* for an "Outside Mount" for windows 35" to 50" in width. For larger or smaller windows see Chapter 2. It is usually necessary to mount the P.M.M. Board* first, so accurate drapery measurements can be obtained.

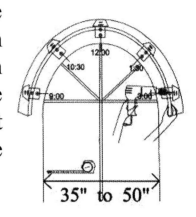

By comparison the "Outside Mount" provides for an overall easier installation than the "Inside Mount". Combining the less pliable P.M.M. Board* with the very pliable P.L. Strip* provides for strength and flexibility. The P.M.M. Board* is applied to the outside of the window frame and held in place by 5 corner irons. There is no direct drapery application to the P.M.M. Board* which makes it easier to maneuver, manage, and mount. The drapes are applied to the pliable P.L. Strip* then velcroed to the top of the P.M.M. Board*. Instructions on how to make and apply the drapes will be detailed in Chapters 4 through 10. It is very important to carefully read the following page regarding warnings and safety instructions.

* Polystyrene Lattice Strip abbreviated as P.L. Strip*
* Polystyrene Moulding Mounting Board abbreviated as P.M.M. Board*

WARNINGS AND SAFETY INSTRUCTIONS

The following safety instructions pertain particularly to the use and inherent properties of the possible breakage of the Polystyrene Moulding Mounting Board (abbreviated as P.M.M.Board*):

(1) **SAFETY GLASSES SHOULD BE WORN AT ALL TIMES BY ALL PERSONS in the work area while handling the P.M.M. Board*.**
(2) **NEVER BALANCE YOURSELF WITH THE P.M.M. BOARD* as should it break you could lose your balance and fall. Always maintain your balance away from the P.M.M. Board*, never leaning on it.**
(3) **NEVER BEND A BARE P.M.M. Board* WITH METAL OBJECTS such as screws or thumbtacks in it, should it break these objects could become projectile. Always have fabric or tape covering the P.M.M. Board* to help catch these objects.**
(4) **The corner irons should always be securely fastened to the wall first and then gently bend the P.M.M. Board* to meet each corner iron and secure with screws. Never try to first put the corner irons in the P.M.M. Board* and then try to bend it in position to be secured to the wall.**
(5) **Do not put any additional holes in it or bend it back and forth before mounting.**
(6) **Do not use the P.M.M. Board* on windows with a width less than 36", or a height greater than 10'.**
(7) **Do not allow children or pets in the work area.**

Overall View

Enlarged side view of the P.M.M. Board*
- Curved side
- Wide side →
- Thin side
- Flat side

Ranch Base P.M.M. Board* 1/2" x 3 1/4"

◎ = # 10 steel flat washer

= # 8 x 5/8" Flat Head Phillips Wood Screw

= Screws in package of corner irons

= Hollow Wall anchor (optional)

= Corner Iron 2 1/2" x 5/8"

If using the /2" x 2 7/16 P.M.M. Board* then use corner irons 2" x 5/8")

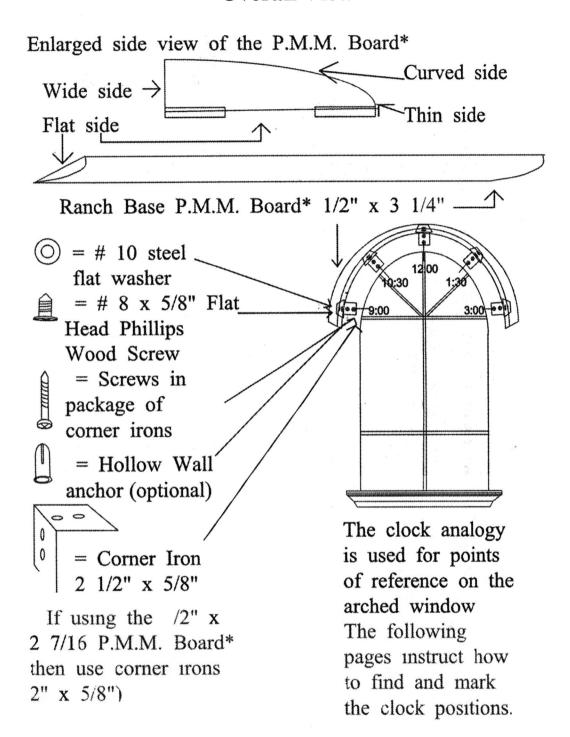

The clock analogy is used for points of reference on the arched window The following pages instruct how to find and mark the clock positions.

Checklist For Tools and Supplies

* Safety glasses
* 1 P.M.M. Board* Ranch Base 1/2"x 3 1/4"
* 2 P.L. Strips*
* Metal tape measure
* Ruler or T-square
* Level
* 1" Masking tape
* 2 packages of 4 corner irons size 2 1/2" x 5/8" (with screws)
* 10 to 14, # 8 x 5/8" Flat head Phillips wood screws
* 5 to 7, # 10 Steel flat washers
* 10 to 14 Hollow wall anchors (optional)
* Electric drill
* Phillips and Flat head screwdriver
* Pencil and Art gum eraser
* Velcro 10'
* Hot glue gun
* Fabric glue
* The desired Drapery treatment instructions

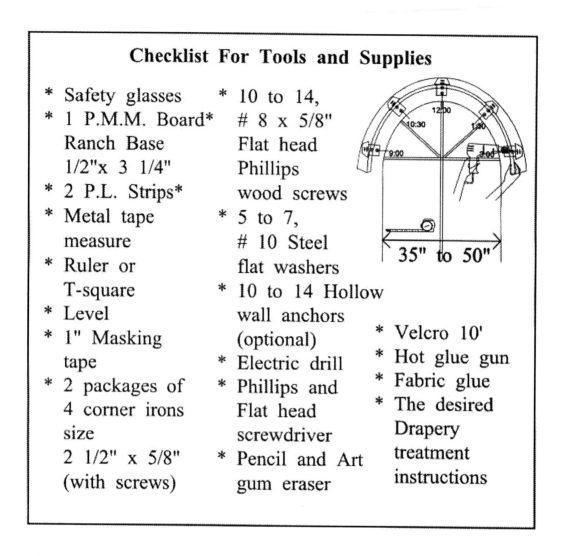

It will be helpful to know ahead of time the window treatment style and how much of the window glass is to be left open. Measure how many inches outside the window edge the window treatment is to hang. Go at least 4" to get past the metal flashing that is around the edges of most windows. If the window width is 50" and it is desired to hang the window treatment father than 4", then see Chapter 2 "Outside Mount for Windows Greater than 51".

(a.) Many of the Palladian windows have an aluminum strip in the middle of the window. This is handy to find the 12:00 o'clock position, which is very important for it to be exactly centered. With a pencil very lightly mark the center (12:00) on the window edge and inside the arch.

(b.) Find the 3:00 and 9:00 positions by measuring from the floor or the horizontal aluminum strip in the window. Lightly mark this spot with a pencil on the window edge and inside the arch.

(c.) The 1:30 and 10:30 positions are halfway between 12:00 and 3:00, and 12:00 and 9:00. To find them use a long strip of masking tape. Start one end of the tape at exactly 12:00 and tape to and follow the inside of the arch to 3:00. Tear it off at exactly 3:00.

(d.) Remove the tape and cut it in half.

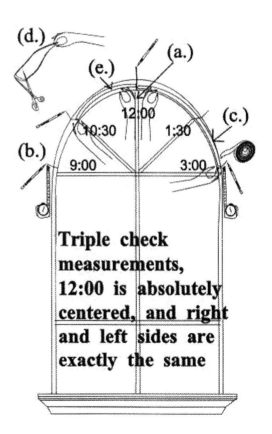

(e.) Start the halved tape at 12:00, tape to and follow the arch. Where it stops is 10:30 on the left side, repeat the same for the right side for 1:30. Lightly mark these positions with a pencil on the window edge and inside the arch, **measure to ensure they are both the same distance from 12:00.**

(a.) Measure how many inches outside the window frame the window treatment is to hang (at least 4"). With a pencil and either a ruler or a T-square lightly draw a straight line from the mark made at the window edge to the desired distance for the window treatment to hang.

(b.) Then turn the ruler sideways (or use the top of the T-square) to lightly draw a line perpendicular to the top of the drawn line.

(c.) Do this at all the clock positions except at 12:00 use a level to draw the perpendicular line to ensure that it is perfectly straight.

(d.) Hold the outer top side of the corner iron perfectly centered and level to the perpendicular lines on the wall. With a pencil, lightly mark the two holes of the corner iron by tracing the edges of the holes. Do this at 12:00, 1:30, 3:00, 10:30 and 9:00. **Be sure 12:00 is absolutely centered.**

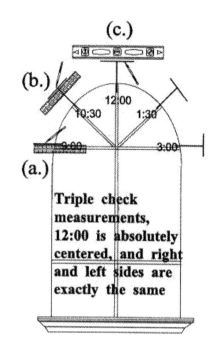

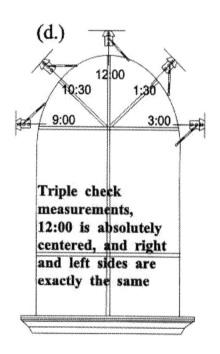

(a.) Ensure that all the holes are the same distance from the window edge and the 12:00 is absolutely centered, and the 1:30 and 10:30 are exactly the same, and the 3:00 and 9:00 are exactly the same. **This is very important because the placement of the corner irons will form the shape of the arch so it will appear symmetrical, otherwise it will look lopsided.**

(b.) Hollow wall anchors are optional, if they are used then predrill pilot holes for the hollow wall anchors as shown at 9:00. Do this for all the clock positions. However if the hollow wall anchors are not used then only predrill very small pilot holes for the screws from the package of corner irons.

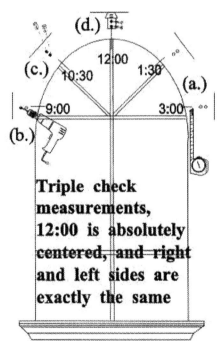

(c.) Insert the hollow wall anchors into the pilot holes as shown at 10:30. Do this to all the clock positions. If they are not used then proceed to (d.) omitting the hollow wall anchors.

(d.) Line up the corner iron to the hollow wall anchors, or pilot holes, and slowly screw in the screws from the package of corner irons as shown at 12:00. Do this to all the clock positions. After all the corner irons have been placed then erase the pencil markings with an art gum eraser.

(a.) To position the "Outside Mount" it is important to find and mark the exact middle of the P.M.M. Board*. This will be the point of reference for any of the drapery treatments so they will appear symmetrical and balanced.

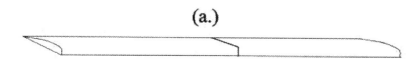

(a.)

(b.) To find the exact middle of the board, measure the entire length of the P.M.M Board* to the nearest 1/8", then divide this number by 2. A calculator may be helpful when dividing fractions of an inch (1/8" = 0.125, 1/4" = 0.25, 1/2" = 0.50), or if there is a metric side of the tape measure, use it for easier calculations. Measure from one end to this divided distance number. (c.) Mark this spot with a pencil, on the flat side, curved side, wide side and the thin side of the P.M.M. Board*, to make viewing the center easier.

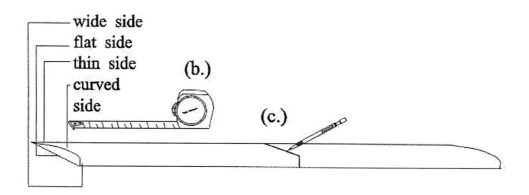

(a.) Locate the exact center of the P.M.M Board*. Place the curved side of the P.M.M. Board* so it will rest on top of the outer top portion of the corner iron at 12:00 o'clock. The flat side is up, the wide side will face out, and the thin side will be next to the wall.

(b.) Line up the center of the P.M.M. Board* to the 12:00 o'clock corner iron holes, and from the underside mark these holes with a pencil.

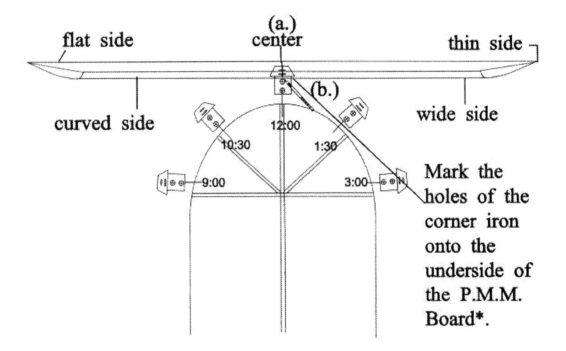

(c.) Remove the P.M.M. Board* and predrill only the first hole as a pilot hole at the pencil mark near the wide side. Use only a very small drill bit for the pilot hole as the threads of the screw should hold the P.M.M. Board* in place.

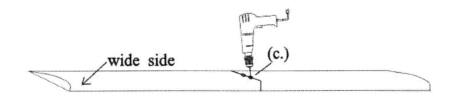

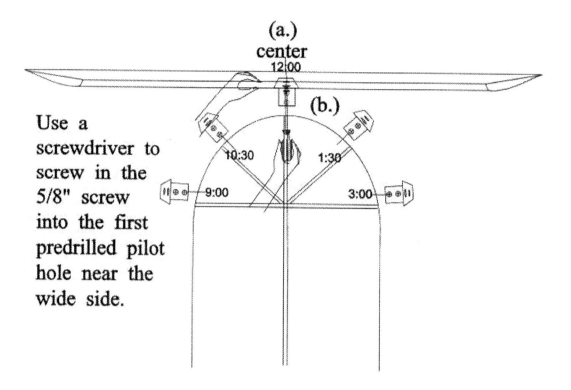

Use a screwdriver to screw in the 5/8" screw into the first predrilled pilot hole near the wide side.

(a.) Replace the P.M.M Board* with the curved side down resting on top of the 12:00 o'clock corner iron. The flat side is up, wide side faces out, and the thin side is next to the wall. (b.) Line up the predrilled hole to the first hole in the 12:00 o'clock corner iron, and screw in the 5/8" screw from the inner top of the corner iron through the outer top, and into the first predrilled pilot hole (near the wide side). As mentioned the very small predrilled pilot holes serve as only a guide for the screws, the threads of the screw should hold the P.M.M. Board*.

Use a hand held or electric screw driver to screw in the screws, because a power drill may strip the screw, and will be too hard to maneuver in the tight upper area of the corner iron.

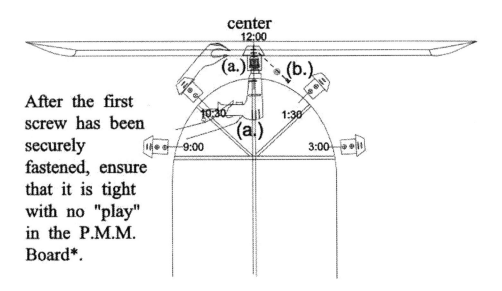

After the first screw has been securely fastened, ensure that it is tight with no "play" in the P.M.M. Board*.

(a.) Steady the P.M.M. Board* and predrill for the second hole of the corner iron near the thin side of the P.M.M. Board*. Again be sure to use a very small drill bit, much smaller than the screws to be used. (b.) After the second hole has been predrilled then use the # 10 steel washer along with the 5/8" screw, and screw it into the second hole. If you predrill both holes of the corner iron at the same time, the second hole is not likely to match up after the first screw has been fastened.

The # 10 steel washer keeps from having too much of the 5/8" screw from protruding through the thin side of the P.M.M. Board*. If too much of the screw still protrudes it should only be a small amount and will be covered by the velcro and should not interfere with the adhesion of the velcro.

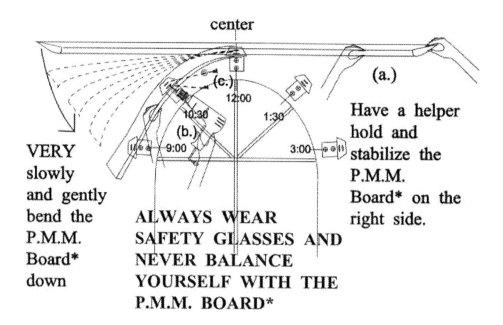

(a.) Have a helper hold the P.M.M. Board on the right side (i.e. 1:30 and 3:00 o'clock) to stabilize the P.M.M. Board*,

(b.) While you very slowly and gently bend it down to the 10:30 position so it will rest flat on top of the 10:30 corner iron. Hold and steady the P.M.M. Board* then predrill a very small pilot hole (much smaller than the screws used) into the first hole of the corner iron near the wide side of the P.M.M. Board*, as done in the 12:00 o'clock corner iron. Continue to hold the P.M.M. Board* in this position and screw in the 5/8" screw into the first hole.

(c.) After the first screw has been fastened then predrill for the second hole of the corner iron near the thin side of the P.M.M. Board* and screw in the 5/8" screw along with the # 10 washer as done in the 12:00 o'clock corner iron.

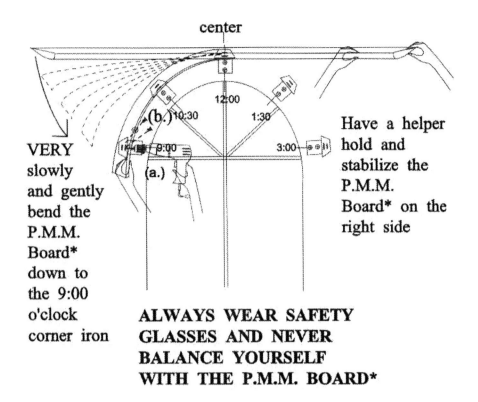

ALWAYS WEAR SAFETY GLASSES AND NEVER BALANCE YOURSELF WITH THE P.M.M. BOARD*

(a.) Again, very gently bend the P.M.M. Board* down until it rests flat on top of the 9:00 o'clock corner iron. Hold the P.M.M. Board* steady, and as done before in the 10:30 and 12:00 o'clock corner irons, predrill a very small pilot hole in the corner iron near the wide side of the P.M.M. Board* and then screw in the 5/8" screw.

(b.) After the first screw has been fastened then predrill for the second hole in the corner iron near the thin side and screw in the 5/8" screw along with the #10 washer as done in the 10:30 and 12:00 o'clock corner irons.

(a.) Now move to the 1:30 corner iron. The P.M.M. Board* may be slightly harder to manipulate but continue to use slow gentle movements to manipulate it flat on top of the corner iron Repeat the procedure done in the 10:30 and 9:00 o'clock corner irons.

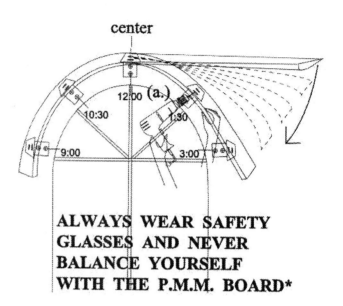

ALWAYS WEAR SAFETY GLASSES AND NEVER BALANCE YOURSELF WITH THE P.M.M. BOARD*

(b.) Again slowly and gently move down to the 3:00 o'clock position and follow the same procedure done in the previous corner irons.

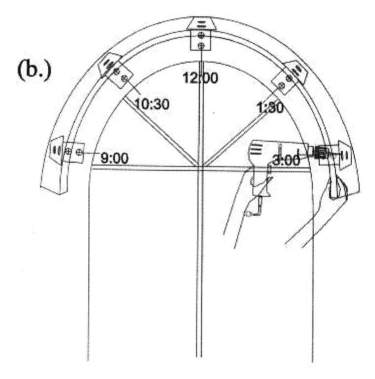

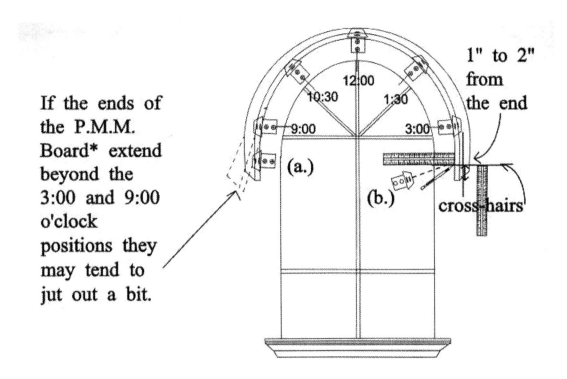

If the ends of the P.M.M. Board* extend beyond the 3:00 and 9:00 o'clock positions they may tend to jut out a bit.

(a.) To correct this apply corner irons at points near the ends of the P.M.M. Board*.

(b.) Position the corner irons at the same distance from the window frame as the rest of the corner irons. Measure how many inches from the window frame that the other corner irons were placed. Measure from the end of the P.M.M. Board* 1" to 2". Mark the spot where these two points meet (crosshairs). This is where to place the end corner irons.

Do not attempt at this time or any other time to put the corner irons in the P.M.M. Board* first, then attach them to the wall. Rather apply the corner irons to the position on the wall and then bend the P.M.M. Board* to meet the corner irons. And as always be sure to wear safety glasses while handling the P.M.M. Board*.

Overview

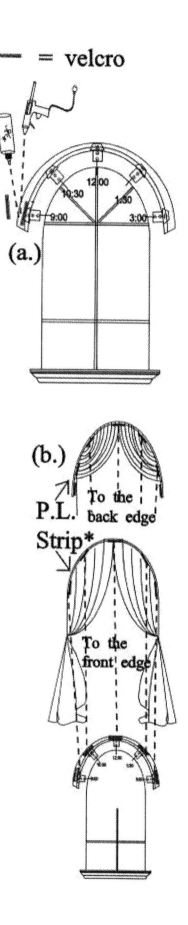

− = velcro

(a.) To the top of the P.M.M. Board* velcro will be applied to marry to velcro applied to the underside of the P.L. strip*. Apply 2 rows of 6" strips of velcro lengthwise to the front and back edges at each of the clock positions and the very ends. For greater ease of repositioning, the velcro can be applied in long strips along the entire front and back edge of the P.M.M. Board*. Use hot glue (preferably), fabric glue, or velcro adhesive in the tube, to provide extra needed adhesion to hold the velcro in place. If you are uncertain of your abilities to handle a hot glue gun while up on a ladder, then use the fabric glue or velcro adhesive in the tube and wait 24 hours to dry.

(b.) The drapery treatment will be applied to the P.L. Strip* with thumbtacks, rod pocket sleeve, or velcro. The P.L. Strip* will then be velcroed to the P.M.M. Board*. Apply the velcro to the underside of the P.L. strip* at all the clock positions and at the very ends. See the desired drapery treatment chapter for specific instructions in how the P.L. Strip* and drapery treatments are applied.

(a.) To secure the very end of the P.L. Strip* to the end of the P.M.M. Board*, slip a strip of 1" masking tape up in the small gap between the wall and the P.M.M. Board*. Wrap the tape completely around the two ends. Here it is shown illustrated without the drapery treatment, but do this after the drapery treatment has been applied.

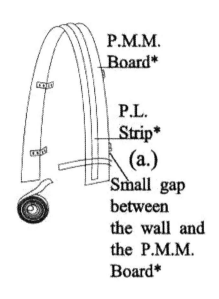

(b.) Regardless of which style of window treatment chosen, all of the hardware and the P.M.M. Board* should be hidden up and out of site under all of the drapery fabric.

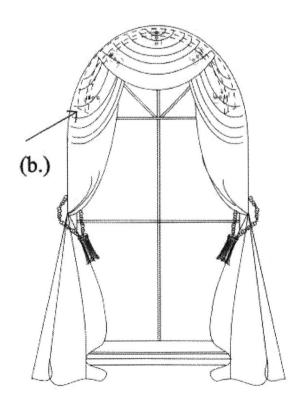

Chapters 4 through 10 will show how to make and apply the drapery panels and top treatments to the P.M.M. Board* and the P.L. Strip*.

Chapter 2
Outside Mount For Windows Larger Than 51"

This chapter deals with how to put two P.M.M. Boards* together to make one longer board for an outside mount of windows larger than 51". Chapter 1 "The Outside Mount" will be referred back to for hardware placement and mounting. For windows smaller than 34" see the subsection at the end of this chapter.

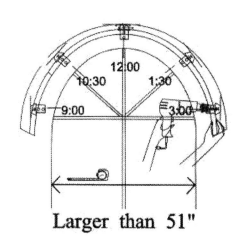

Larger than 51"

For windows larger than 51" the P.M.M. Board* will need to be made longer. This is done by joining two P.M.M. Boards* together with 2 mending plates. One end of each of the P.M.M. Boards* will be cut with a hacksaw to length, so that the other end will be the clean and smooth factory cut end that will abut next to each other. This is also done so that where the P.M.M. Boards* are joined with the mending plate, it will be at the top of the arch where the mending plate can be attached to the 12:00 o'clock corner iron. **See the Warnings and Safety instructions on page 2.** Safety glasses should be worn by all persons in the work area.

* Polystyrene Lattice Strip abbreviated as P.L. Strip*
* Polystyrene Moulding Mounting Board abbreviated as P.M.M. Board*

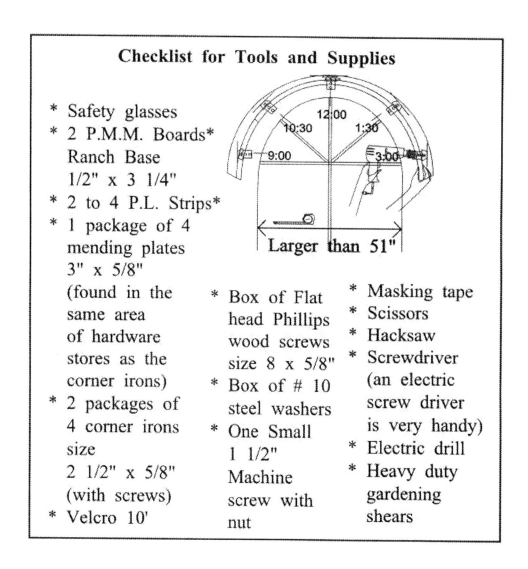

Checklist for Tools and Supplies

* Safety glasses
* 2 P.M.M. Boards*
  Ranch Base
  1/2" x 3 1/4"
* 2 to 4 P.L. Strips*
* 1 package of 4
  mending plates
  3" x 5/8"
  (found in the
  same area
  of hardware
  stores as the
  corner irons)
* 2 packages of
  4 corner irons
  size
  2 1/2" x 5/8"
  (with screws)
* Velcro 10'
* Box of Flat
  head Phillips
  wood screws
  size 8 x 5/8"
* Box of # 10
  steel washers
* One Small
  1 1/2"
  Machine
  screw with
  nut
* Masking tape
* Scissors
* Hacksaw
* Screwdriver
  (an electric
  screw driver
  is very handy)
* Electric drill
* Heavy duty
  gardening
  shears

The Ranch Base P.M.M. Board* 1/2" x 3 1/4" is used for making the new longer P.M.M. Board*. Occasionally this P.M.M. Board* can be found in 10' lengths, carefully measure the arch and see if it may be possible to use one 10' board. Review the entire chapter to gain a full understanding before installation.

Overall View

Two P.M.M. Boards* of the same kind the Ranch Base 1 /2" x 3 1 /4" are used.

(a.) One end of each of the P.M.M. Boards* will need to be cut with a hacksaw, so that the factory cut end of each P.M.M. Board* will be available to be abutted up to each other.

(b.) The two factory ends will then be attached on the flat side of the P.M.M. Board* by two mending plates, 3" x 5/8". Use the shorter screws from the box of Flat Head Phillips Wood Screws size 8 x 5/8" and the # 10 steel washers, so as to not have too much of the screw protruding through the P.M.M. Board*.

(c.) The machine screw and washer is applied to the flat side, and is secured underneath the 12:00 o'clock corner iron with a nut.

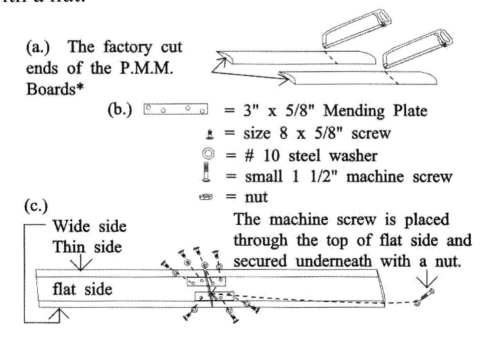

To find out how much to cut from each end of the P.M.M. Boards*, first measure the arch. Decide how much "off the glass" that is desired for the window treatment.

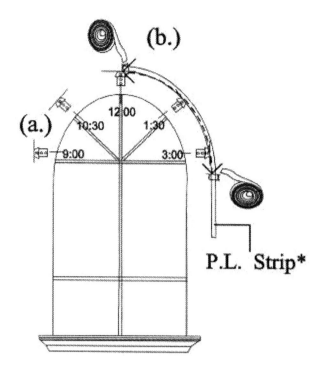

(a.) Place the corner irons the desired distance outside the arch as directed in Chapter 1 "The Outside <u>Mount</u>" pages 5 through 7. After placing the corner irons, use masking tape and the P.L. Strip* to measure the arch so as much as possible of the arch can beclosely approximated.

(b.) Tape the one end of the P.L. Strip* to the 12:00 o'clock corner iron and have it follow the arch along the top of the 1:30 and 3:00 o'clock corner irons to a point roughly 3" to 6" past the 3:00 corner iron, mark this spot with a piece of masking tape.

(c.) Remove the P.L. Strip* and measure this distance marked by the masking tape with a metal tape measure.

(d.) Measure, mark, and cut this same distance of length for each of the P.M.M. Boards*.

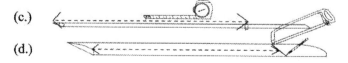

(a.) To form the new longer P.M.M. Board*, place the factory cut ends of the P.M.M. Boards* together, with the thin sides together, wide sides together, and the flat side up. The P.M.M. Boards* have been shortened for viewing purposes.

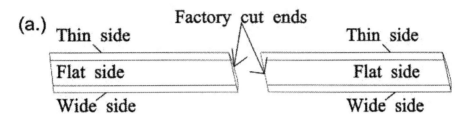

(b.) Locate the inside ridges of the P.M.M. Boards*, carefully line them up, the mending plates will be specifically placed inside of them.

(c.) Place masking tape to the outside of the ridges to help hold the P.M.M. Boards* in place while they are worked on. Be sure the P.M.M. Boards* are as close as possible to each other.

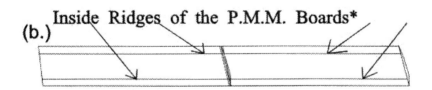

Place strips of masking tape outside of the ridges to help hold the P.M.M. Boards* together.

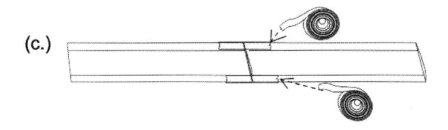

(a.) Place the exact middle of one of the 3" mending plate to the exact middle of where the two P.M.M. Boards* meet, immediately next to the inside ridge on the thin side of the P.M.M. Boards*.

(b.) Place the other 3" mending plate immediately next to the inside ridge on the wide side of the P.M.M. Boards*, so that the second hole lines up perfectly to the exact middle of where the two P.M.M. Boards* meet, so that you can see the P.M.M. Boards* meeting in the middle of this second hole. This is where it will attach to the 12:00 o'clock corner iron so the new longer P.M.M. Board* will be perfectly symmetrical. This will leave one hole for one P.M.M. Board*, and two holes for the other P.M.M. Board*.

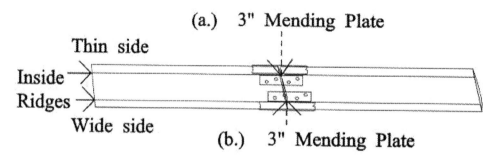

(c.) Predrill very small pilot holes (much smaller than the # 8 x 5/8" screws that are used) for all holes except the second hole of the 3" mending plate that falls exactly in the middle.

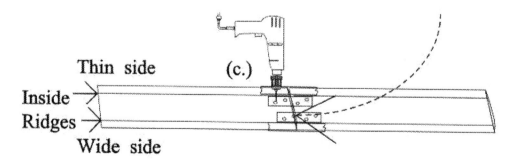

(a.) Place the size 8 x 5/8" phillips wood screws along with the # 10 steel washers into the predrilled smaller holes. The predrilled smaller holes serve only as guiding pilot holes for the wood screws, the threads of the wood screws should catch and hold the P.M.M. Board*. This will be for all the holes except the second hole of the 3" mending plate that falls exactly in the middle of where the two P.M.M. Boards* meet.

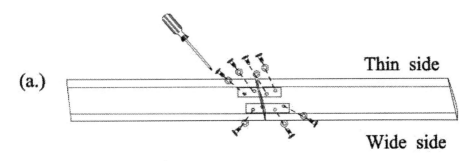

(b.) Now predrill for the second hole of the 3" mending plate, that falls exactly in the middle of where the two P.M.M. Boards* meet. Predrill this hole large enough for the 1 1/2" machine screw to pass through easily from the flat side completely through to the curved side of the P.M.M. Board*. This machine screw will pass through the P.M.M. Board* and through the first hole of the 12:00 corner iron and will be held in place with the nut.

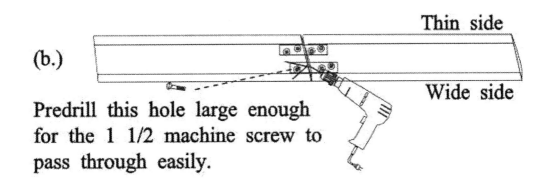

Predrill this hole large enough for the 1 1/2 machine screw to pass through easily.

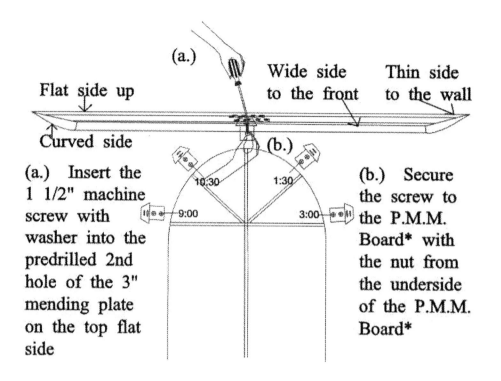

Place the P.M.M. Board* with the flat side up and the curved side down resting on top of the 12:00 o'clock corner iron.

(a.) Line up the predrilled second hole of the 3" mending plate to the first hole in the 12:00 o'clock corner iron, and insert the 1 1/2" machine screw along with the # 10 steel washer, from the top of the P.M.M. Board* from the flat side through to the curved side and through to the first hole of the corner iron.

(b.) Secure the P.M.M. Board* to the corner iron with the machine screw, and apply the nut to the machine screw from the underside (curved side) of the P.M.M. Board*.

ALWAYS WEAR SAFETY GLASSES AND NEVER USE THE P.M.M. BOARD* TO BALANCE YOURSELF.

The mending plate provides extra strength to the P.M.M. Board*, and since this is for an outside mount greater than 51 ", an arch of this size should not be too severe, however if you are not sure of your capabilities to gently bend the P.M.M. Board* without breaking it, should the mending plates become projectile, (a.) then apply masking tape to the mending plate and screws after it has been mounted to the 12:00 o'clock position and before manipulating the P.M.M. Board* to the other corner irons. And as always wear safety glasses.

After the P.M.M. Board* has been completely mounted and secured to all of the corner irons and there is no bending movement of the P.M.M. Board*, then gently remove the masking tape that is over the mending plates. This is done so that there will not be any interference with the adhesion of the velcro to the 12:00 o'clock position.

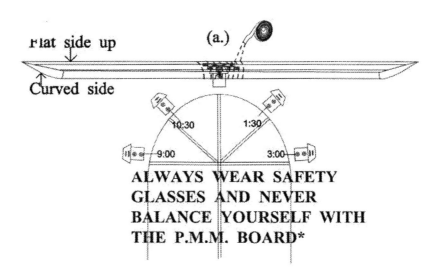

Now follow the general directions as outlined in Chapter 1 "The Outside Mount", pages 12 through 16. The mending plate site will be a bit more stiff than the rest of the P.M.M. Board*. As in "The Outside Mount" for windows without the mending plates gently manipulate the P.M.M. Board* being careful not to use force, and then hold this postion while it is predrilled and the screws are placed into the corner irons.

(a.) This is especially so for the two corner irons which follow directly after the mending plates (1:30 and 10:30 positions).
(b.) If the P.M.M Board* bows out a little after the mending plates, it will be alright as long as both sides bow out the same amount at the same position in the arch, to provide for symmetry.

The following pages will address how to make the P.L. Strip* longer so that it can be attached to the new longer P.M.M. Board*.

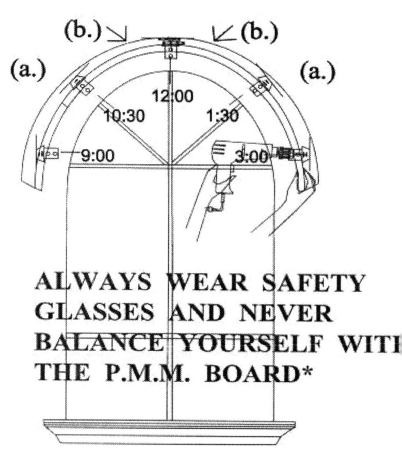

Overall View

The drapes will be applied to the thin and very pliable P.L. Strip*, which is then velcroed on top of the P.M.M. Board*. To make the P.L. Strip* longer is relatively easy, involving only cutting the P.L. Strip* and taping it together with masking tape. The P.L. Strip* cuts very easy, a pair of heavy duty gardening shears, or the like works very well.

The P.L. Strip* is cut and joined together in a different way than the P.M.M. Board*. This is so that the thickness of where it is joined together will not be at the 12:00 o'clock position where the velcro is placed (the velcro and the thickness of the joined together P.L. Strip* would make this area too thick).

(a.) The 1st P.L. Strip* will remain whole and the 2nd P.L. Strip* will be cut into 4 pieces (2 large and 2 small pieces).

(b.) The two smaller pieces will act as splints to hold the 2 larger pieces to the ends of the 1st P.L. Strip*, secured with masking tape.

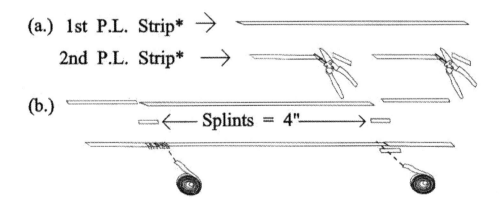

To find out how much to cut off of the second P.L. Strip*, use the measurement that was obtained for the P.M.M. Board* as shown below, only this measurement will be used differently.

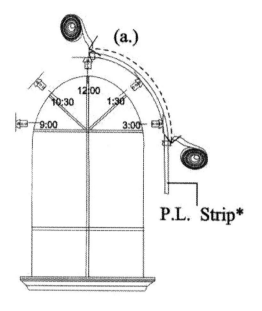

(a.) Tape one end of the P.L. Strip* to the 12:00 o'clock corner iron and have it follow the arch along the top of the 1:30 and 3:00 o'clock corner irons to a point roughly 3" to 6" past the 3:00 corner iron, mark this spot with a piece of masking tape.

(a.) Remove the P.L. Strip* and measure this distance marked by the masking tape with a metal tape measure. Multiply this measurement x 2 for the total arch measurement.

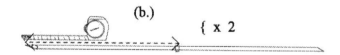

(a.) Measure the exact length of the first P.L. Strip*, some may vary slightly in length, subtract the length of the P.L. Strip* from the (b.) total measurement taken of the arch, then divide this number by two, this is how much that will need to be cut off of each of the ends of the second P.L. Strip*.

(c.) For example the total arch measurement is 120" and the length of the 1st P.L. Strip* is 96", then 120 - 96 = 24, then 24 divided by 2 = 12, (d.) you would then cut 12" off each of the ends of the second P.L. Strip*. (e.) With the piece that is left over, cut two 4" strips for the splints

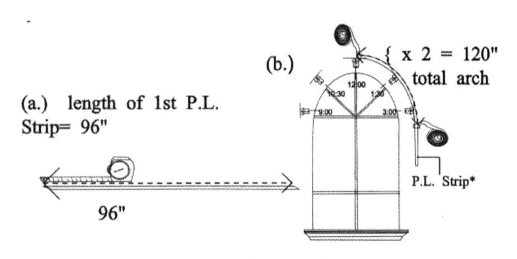

(c.) 120" - 96" = 24"; 24" divided by 2 = 12"

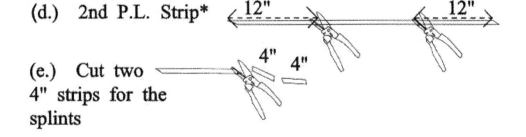

The 4" strips, which will serve as splints, are placed on what will become the underside of the P.L. Strip*.

(a.) First tape 2 inches of the 4" strip to one end of the 96" uncut P.L. Strip*, start taping at the end closest to the middle of the uncut P.L. Strip*.

(b.) After the first 2 inches of the 4" strip has been secured to the uncut P.L. Strip* then place the 12" strip of P.L. Strip* next to the uncut P.L. Strip* and on top of the remaining 2 inches of the 4" splint and continue taping the rest of the splint, so a bond is formed by the masking tape. Try not to make more than a single series of passes of the tape, so as to not build up any unnecessary thickness. Repeat the same for the other end of the uncut P.L. Strip*.

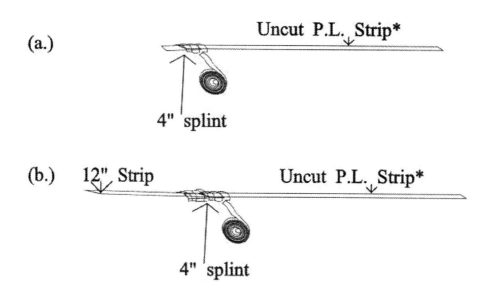

(a.) Just as directed in Chapter 1 "The Outside Mount" page 8, on how to find the exact middle of the P.M.M Board*, find the middle of the new longer P.L. Strip*. Follow the general directions as outlined in Chapter 1 "The Outside Mount", except make allowances for the thickness under the joined area on the P.L. Strip* by not putting any velcro under this area as well as the coordinating area of the P.M.M. Board* to which the P.L. Strip* will attach.

(b.) To find this area on the P.M.M. Board* place the P.L. Strip* through a dry test run, lining up the middle of the P.L. Strip* to the middle of the new longer P.M.M. Board*.

(c.) To temporarily hold the P.L. Strip* in place either have a helper hold the ends of the P.L. Strip* in place or use masking tape. With a pencil mark the area on the P.M.M. Board* where the joined area of P.L. Strip* lays.

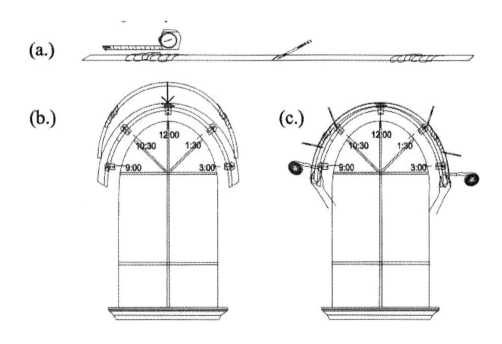

(a.) Mark the area above and below the joined areas of the P.L. Strip* to coordinate as close possible to the 1:30, 10:30, 3:00, and 9:00 o'clock positions on both the P.L. Strip* and the P.M.M. Board*. Make different marking so as to indicate where to place the 6" strips of velcro that will marry the P.L. Strip* to the P.M.M. Board*.

(b.) Apply velcro to the 12:00 o'clock, and to the marked areas above and below the joined areas of the P.L. Strip* after the drapery fabric has been applied to the P.L. Strip*. Below it is shown with the velcro already in place, but the velcro should be applied only after the drapery fabric has been applied to the P.L. Strip*. Follow the directions in the drapery chapters in how to apply the drapery fabric to the P.L. Strip*. Use the marking made when placing the velcro on top of the drapery fabric.

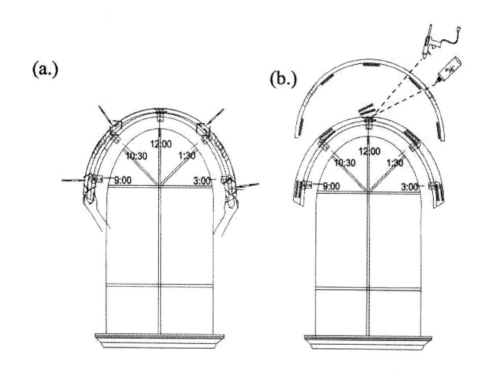

For Windows 34" or Less

For windows 34" or less the arch is too small and the bending pressure too severe for the P.M.M. Board* to be used. However the P.L. Strip* can be used by making a few changes.

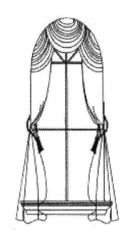

The depth of the projection of the window treatment will be much less than with the P.M.M. Board*. The drapery material used should be fairly thin and light weight, especially if the windows are tall and the treatment will be full length to the floor. Much smaller corner irons will need to be used and the screws should be place through the top of the P.L. Strip* and through the top of the corner iron and fastened underneath the corner iron with a nut. Also you will need to put in additional corner irons. These additional corner irons can be placed at 12:00, 1:00, 2:00, 3:00, 11:00, 10:00, and 9:00 o'clock. Mount the P.L. Strip* as if it were the P.M.M. Board and apply both the drapery panels and the top treatment to another P.L. Strip* and velcro it on top of the mounted P.L. Strip*.

Follow the basic instructions as outlined in Chapter 1 "The Outside Mount", including the Safety Instructions, except substitute the thin P.L. Strip* for the "Ranch Base" P.M.M. Board*. Safety glasses are still required for all persons in the work area.

Chapter 3
The Inside Mount

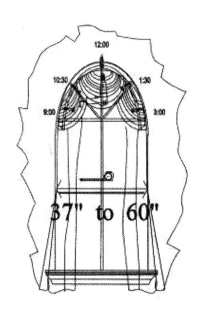

This chapter deals with the Inside Mount for windows 37" to 60". For windows smaller than 36" see the following subsection at the end of this chapter. For window larger than 60" an inside mount may not be possible, using the mending plates may prove to be too difficult to manage, occasionally 10 foot Ranch Base P.M.M. Boards* can be found in large hardware stores. The inside mount is a much more difficult window treatment to do than the outside mount and should be left to the experienced craftsman. In addition to being harder to manage and more prone to breakage, it requires a minimum of at least two people to mount, and a great deal of strength from the person who holds the P.M.M. Board* in place. Also this person must be tall enough to be able to stand on the floor and hold the P.M.M. Board* into position, as it will be unsafe to stand up on a ladder while holding and pushing the drapery ladden P.M.M. Board* up into the inside of the window frame. As always safety glasses are required, see the safety and warning instructions on the following page.

* Polystyrene Lattice Strip abbreviated as P.L. Strip*
* Polystyrene Moulding Mounting Board abbreviated as P.M.M. Board*

WARNINGS AND SAFETY INSTRUCTIONS

The following safety instructions pertain particularly to the use and inherent properties of the possible breakage of the Polystyrene Moulding Mounting Board (abbreviated as P.M.M.Borard*):

(1) **SAFETY GLASSES SHOULD BE WORN AT ALL TIMES BY ALL PERSONS in the work area while handling the P.M.M. Board*.**
(2) **NEVER BALANCE YOURSELF WITH THE P.M.M. BOARD* as should it break you could lose your balance and fall. Always maintain your balance away from the P.M.M. Board*, never leaning on it.**
(3) **NEVER BEND A BARE P.M.M. Board* WITH METAL OBJECTS such as screws or thumbtacks in it, should it break these objects could become projectile. Always have fabric or tape covering the P.M.M. Board* to help catch these objects.**
(4) **The corner irons should always be securely fastened to the wall first and then gently bend the P.M.M. Board* to meet each corner iron and secure with screws. Never try to first put the corner irons in the P.M.M. Board* and then try to bend it in position to be secured to the wall.**
(5) **Do not put any additional holes in it or bend it back and forth before mounting.**
(6) **Do not use the P.M.M. Board* on windows with a width less than 36", or a height greater than 10'.**
(7) **Do not allow children or pets in the work area.**

Overall view

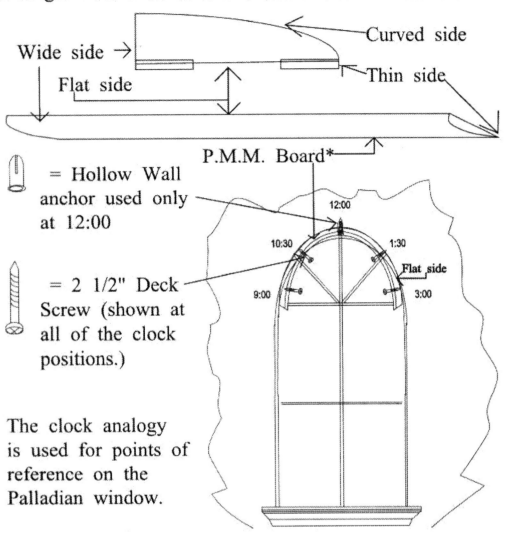

Enlarged side view of the "Ranch Base" P.M.M. Board*

= Hollow Wall anchor used only at 12:00

= 2 1/2" Deck Screw (shown at all of the clock positions.)

The clock analogy is used for points of reference on the Palladian window.

To show the hardware of the "Inside Mount" it is shown without the drapery fabric. The drapery panels and the top treatment will need to be applied to the P.M.M. Board* before mounting.

Checklist For Tools and Supplies

* Safety glasses
* Metal tape measure
* One hollow wall anchor
* 5 to 7, 2 1/2" Deck screws
* Sissors
* Pencil
* Electric drill
* 2 P.M.M. Boards* either Ranch Base, 1/2" x 3 1/4" or 1/2" x 2 7/16"
* Chapter instructions for the top treatment and drapery panel treatment
* Thumbtacks
* Upholstery nails

The Inside Mount uses only the less pliable P.M.M. Board* (while in comparison the outside mount uses the less pliable P.M.M. Board* in conjunction with the very pliable P.L. Strip*). Having less pliability, there is an increase chance of breakage, so have at least one extra P.M.M. Board* on hand should it break.

The drapery panels and top treatment will need to be made first before mounting the "Inside Mount", see the desired window treatment chapter for instructions. Suggested treatment is to apply the drapery panels to the P.M.M. Board* using the rod pocket sleeve as directed in Chapter 5, and apply the top treatment over the rod pocket sleeve using thumbtacks or upholstery nails. Read through this chapter first to gain an understanding of how the treatment will be applied to the P.M.M. Board*.

(a.) To position the Inside Mount it is important to find and mark the exact middle of the P.M.M. Board* because this will be the point of reference for any of the drapery treatments so they will appear symmetrical and balanced.

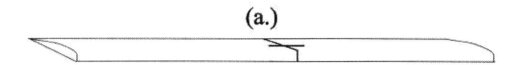

(a.)

(b.) To find the exact middle of the P.M.M. Board*, measure the entire length of the P.M.M. Board* to the nearest 1/8", then divide this number by 2. A calculator may be helpful when dividing fractions of an inch (1/8" = 0.125, 1/4" = 0.25, 1/2" = 0.50), or if there is a metric side of the tape measure, use it for easier calculations. (c.) Measure from one end this divided distance, and mark this spot with a pencil, on the flat side, curved side, wide side and the thin side of the P.M.M. Board*. Find the middle of the width of the board in the same fashion. At the cross hairs where the middle of the length and the width meet make a small dot.

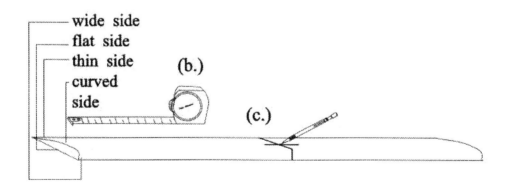

(a.) Predrill a pilot hole, where the small dot was made, make it large enough for a screw to pass through.

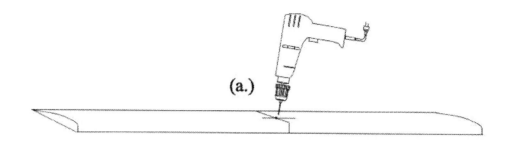

(b.) Now find the center (12:00 o'clock) of the window frame at the top of the half round arch. A lot of windows have an aluminum strip in the middle of the glass pane, which is helpful for finding the center. Mark this spot with a pencil on the window edge and inside the arch. **Ensure that it is absolutely centered.**

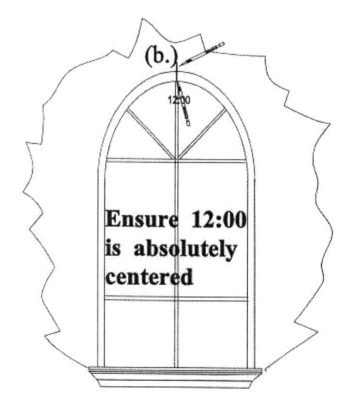

(a.) Put the P.M.M. Board* through a dry test run, up in the window frame. Very gently push the P.M.M. Board* up into the window frame with the flat side up and flush with the sheet rock The wide side of the P.M.M. Board* faces out and the thin side is facing the glass pane. Line up the middle of the P.M.M. Board* and the middle of the window frame.

(b.) Have a partner mark the 3:00 and the 9:00 spots and if possible the 1:30 and the 10:30 spots on the P.M.M. Board*.

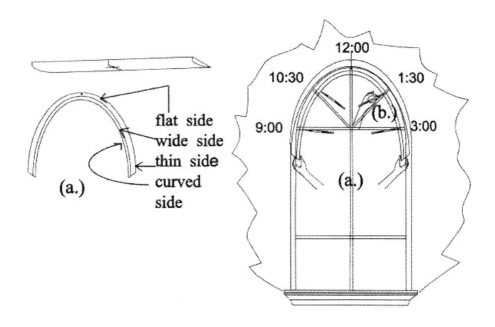

When putting the P.M.M. Board* through the dry test run (or at any other time), DO NOT BEND THE P.M.M. BOARD* BACK AND FORTH! Bend the P.M.M. Board* slowly and gently, and only bend it with the flat side up.

Carefully remove the P.M.M. Board* and

(a.) Readjust the pencil markings so that the left side markings (10:30 and 9:00) and the right side markings (1:30 and 3:00) are equal distance from the center (12:00 o'clock).

(b.) Find the center of the width of the P.M.M. Board* at 1:30, 3:00, 9:00, and 10:30 and predrill a pilot hole large enough for a screw to pass through as done in the 12:00 o'clock position.

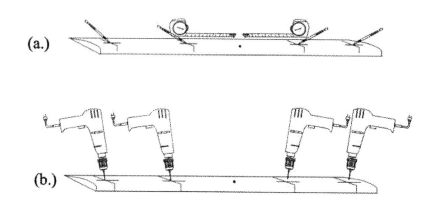

If the ends of the P.M.M. Board* extend more than a few inches past the 3:00 and 9:00 o'clock spots then additional holes can be made into the middle width of the P.M.M. Board* approximately two inches from the very ends of it.

The curtains look and hang best when the P.M.M. Board* is positioned where the front edge of the P.M.M. Board* extends only slightly (1/4" to 1/2") beyond the window frame.

(a.) Again, with the flat side up, gently put the P.M.M. Board* through a perfect dry run. Have a helper **exactly line up the middle of the P.M.M. Board* to the exact middle of the window.** Extend the front edge of the P.M.M. Board* slightly beyond the window frame's edge.

(b.) With a much smaller drill bit than the screw size, drill through the 12:00 o'clock hole that was previously made in the P.M.M. Board* so it goes through the P.M.M. Board* and makes a hole in the interior portion of the window frame in to the sheet rock. CAUTION: MOST WINDOWS HAVE A SMALL EDGE OF METAL FLASHING AROUND THE WINDOW EDGE, BE SURE TO GET PAST THIS METAL FLASHING. Only a small hole is needed at this time.

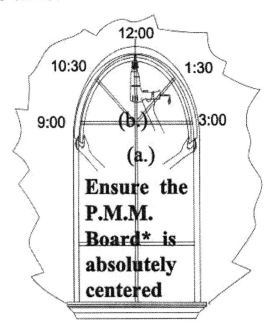

(a.) Remove the P.M.M. Board*. If the pilot hole in the sheet rock of the window's frame is not already large enough to insert the hollow wall anchor, then drill the same pilot hole again. Make it large enough to only be a guide to insert the hollow wall anchor. The 12:00 o'clock is the only hole in which a hollow wall anchor will be used.

(b.) Insert the hollow wall anchor into the center pilot hole inside the window frame.

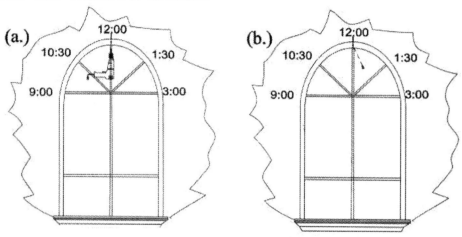

(c.) To apply the window treatment, first apply the drapery panels to the P.M.M. Board*. **Make the rod pocket sleeve large enough to fit the P.M.M. Board*,** see Chapter 5 for basic instructions. Place the panels on the P.M.M. Board* as they will hang in the finished treatment. Put only a small thumbtack at just a few inches on both side of 12:00 and at just a few inches above 3:00 and 9:00, to keep the sleeve from slipping off the P.M.M. Board *.

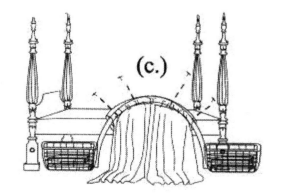

(a.) See Chapter 7 or 8 for basic swag treatment application, except the swags will lay directly over the drapery panels on the P.M.M. Board* instead of a separate P.L. Strip*. Do not use the "Swag Lattice Turned Over" method. Secure the swags over the drapery panels with upholstery nails, do not put them near the holes drilled in the P.M.M. Board* (this will increase the chance of breaking it). AS ALWAYS BE SURE TO WEAR SAFETY GLASSES.

(b.) If tabs for the swags were used, make sure they are placed far enough back on the P.M.M. Board* so they do not show when it is mounted. See page 110 (a.) and (b.) to be sure the sides of the panels are in place prior to mounting. **Triple check to be sure the swags and panels are perfectly centered and lay smooth and neat because it will not be possible to readjust the curtains after they have been mounted.**

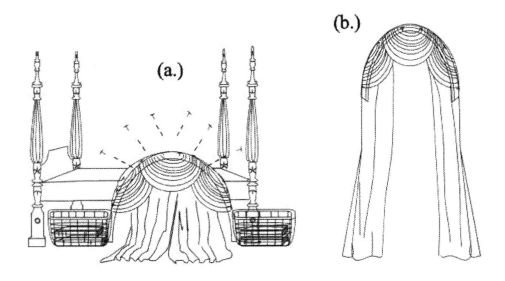

At least two people will be needed to hang the curtains. After the curtains are in place, the P.M.M. Board* will be much heavier. Carefully snip tiny holes in the fabric at the site of the predrilled holes in the P.M.M. Board*, so screws can easily pass through. Apply a small amount of "Fray Stop" (or similar product) at the snip to discourage unraveling of the threads. Place the screws through the fabric and barely through the P.M.M. Board*.

(a.) Have helper gently push the P.M.M. Board* up into the arched window frame until the 12:00 o'clock screw in the P.M.M. Board* lines up with the center hollow wall anchor inside the window frame.

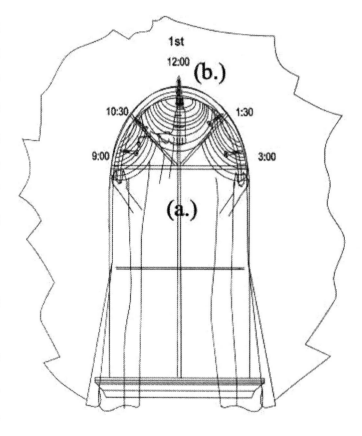

(b.) Carefully screw in the 12:00 o'clock, 2 1/2" deck screw into the center hollow wall anchor. Do not tighten the screw down quite all the way, so you will have just a little give to keep manipulating the P.M.M. Board*. Later you can come back and tighten up all the screws.

(a.) Have helper continue to gently but firmly push the P.M.M. Board* up into the window's inside frame making it fit snugly into the 10:3 0 and the 1:30 positions.

(b.) Next screw the 2 1/2" deck screw first into the 10:30 position and then into the 1:30 position and then finally into the 3:00 and the 9:00 o'clock positions. If your P.M.M. Board* extends past the 3:00 and 9:00 o'clock positions, and if it seems necessary and there are predrilled holes 2 inches from the end, then screw in these positions as well. Go back and tighten up the 12:00 o'clock and any other positions as needed.

(c.) Apply tie backs for a finished and polished look.

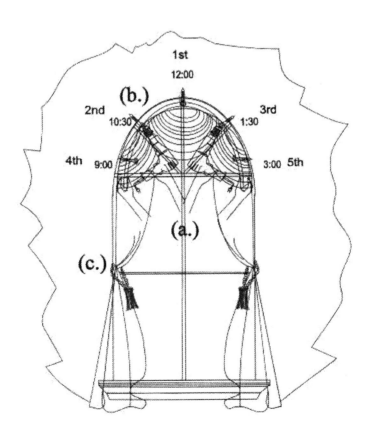

After the curtains have been hung, some light holes may be visible during the day. Light holes appear when the sun shines through and creates spots of light at the perimeter of the arch where the P.M.M. Board* may have not been completely flushed with the inside of the window frame.

(a.) These light holes can be plugged with pieces of a soft sponge cut into strips and gently wedged in the slot between the drapery panel and the under side of the top treatment, so that the curtain is pushed up and nestled next to the inside of the window frame, preventing any light from penetrating.

(b.) Gently wedge the strips of the sponge in the slot underneathe swags or top treatment, inbetween the swags and drapery panel, where they lie on top of the P.M.M. Board*. Use a small flat head screw driver and very little force to push the sponge into this slot.

This should take care of any light holes. At the clock positions where the screws attach the P.M.M. Board* to the inside of the window, it will not be possible to wedge in the strips of the sponge. However this should not present a problem since there should not be light holes in this area.

For Windows Less than 36"

For windows less than 36 inches, the arch will be too severe to bend the P.M.M. Board*. You may find it easier to use the traditional clear plastic rods typically used for sheers.

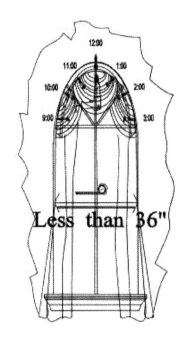

However you can quite successfully use the P.L. Strip* by making a few changes. The drapery material used should be fairly light weight, especially if the windows are tall and the treatment will be full length to the floor. There will not be enough room on the P.L. Strip* to extend the P.L. Strip* past the widow frame's edge, and the mount will need to be flushed or slightly inside the window edge (clearing the 1" metal strip that is with in the sheet rock). Also you will probably need to put in additional screws, depending on how heavy the fabric is, these additional screws can be placed at 12:00, 1:00, 2:00, 3:00, 11:00, 10:00, and 9:00 o'clock.

Follow the basic instructions as outlined in this Chapter "The Inside Mount", substituting the thin P.L. Strip* for the Ranch Base P.M.M. Board*. Safety glasses are still required for all persons in the work area.

Chapter 4
No Sew Gathered Sheet Drapes with Covered Jute Webbing or a Simply Covered Crinoline

This chapter shows how to make no sew drapes, from ordinary bed linens. Also drapery fabrics, and standard size store bought drapes can be used with this window treatment as well.

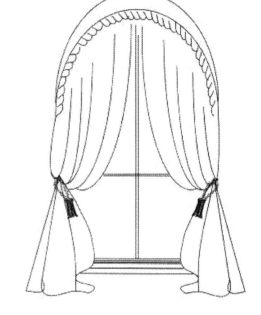

If your windows are taller than average, and taller than the length of say, one twin sheet, we will show you a piecing together technique to conquer this dilemma, involving the use of bishop sleeves and a stationary window treatment. This same technique shows how to make no sew alterations to transform standard 84" store bought drapes into custom made drapes, for today's lofty arched windows.

* Polystyrene Lattice Strip abbreviated as P.L. Strip*
* Polystyrene Moulding Mounting Board abbreviated as P.M.M. Board*

Check List for for Tools and Supplies

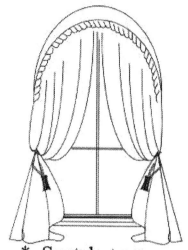

* 5 to 9 Twin sheets or 2 to 4 Queen/King sheets, plus at least one extra twin sheet
* Jute Webbing (yardage = length of P.M.M. Board*)
* Cording Trim with webbed edge for yardage (same as above + 6")
* 2 Tassled tie back holders
* 1 & 1/2 yards Heat and Bond off the bolt
* one to two rolls of 3/4" Heat and Bond
* 2" Masking tape
* 2 Cup hooks or nails
* Fabric glue
* Hot glue gun
* Scotch tape
* Velcro adhesive in the tube
* Velcro 10'
* 2 Heavy cans of food
* Iron
* String
* Sissors
* Tape measure
* Steam iron

To substitute the Simply Covered Crinoline for the Covered Jute Webbing see page 79.

The following pages address the substitutions of drapery fabrics and store bought drapery panels, for the twin sheets.

Yardage Estimation for Drapery Fabric Substitution of Twin sheets

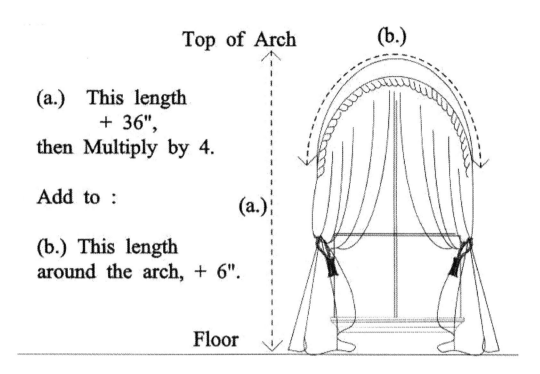

(a.) This length + 36", then Multiply by 4.

Add to :

(b.) This length around the arch, + 6".

(a.) You can substitute one width of Drapery Fabric for one Twin sheet. To obtain the yardage needed for this window treatment, measure from the top of the P.M.M. Board* to the floor, plus add 1 extra yard (36 inches) for puddling, tie backs, and or bishop sleeves. Take this number and multiply by 4 for double fullness.

(b.) After multiplying by 4, then add the length of the P.M.M. Board*, plus 6", to get the total amount of yards needed. To get the yardage figure, divide the number of inches by 36 and round up to the next 1/4 of a yard to know what to tell your fabric store sales person. You will be joining two widths of the fabric together for double fullness. Follow the same basic directions for "No Sew Gathered Sheet Drapes". To cut the drapery fabric see pages 95 and 96.

Custom Look for Store Bought Drapes

1 panel for the top arch (Covered Jute Webbing) + 4 panels for the top half + 4 panels for the bottom half = Total 9 panels for "pieced together" double fullness drapes.

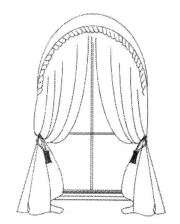

Store bought drapes can be substituted for the twin sheets. Each drapery panel, will equal one twin sheet. If your windows are taller than the standard length of drapery panels (84"), then you can follow the piecing together technique outlined in this chapter. If using the piecing together technique, you will need 9 drapery panels, for double fullness. Four on each side of the window, and one more to make the top of the window treatment.

See the section later in this chapter titled "No Sew Customized Store Bought Drapes" page 89, to see how to alter the drapes, and then follow the same basic directions for "No Sew Gathered Sheet Drapes".

Directions for No Sew Gathered Sheet Drapes (for an unlined drapery panel)

This is for an unlined drapery panel, to add lining see page 60

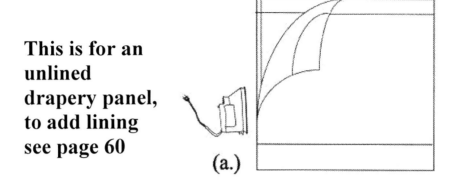

(a.) Use brand new sheets and don't wash them, iron out the creases made by packaging. If using twin sheets, then heat and bond the two sheets together on one side. Keep right sides together, top to top, and bottom to bottom. Use 3/4" Heat and Bond for easy application. (One King sheet can be used in place of two twin sheets.)

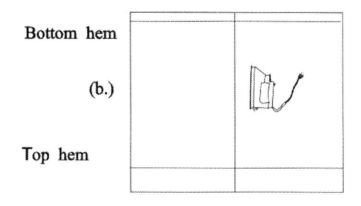

(b.) Open and press seam flat, don't open the seam too much, or it will open it to the adhesive strip of the Heat and Bond.

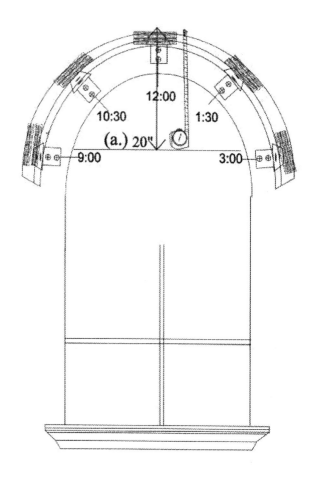

First, mount the P.M.M. Board*, see Chapter 1.

(a.) Measure from the imaginary straight line, just above the 3:00 and 9:00 o'clock position (of the clock analogy), on the half round window. This is where the window first starts to straighten out the curve. Measure to the top highest point of the arch, at 12:00 o'clock. Example: this figure is 20".

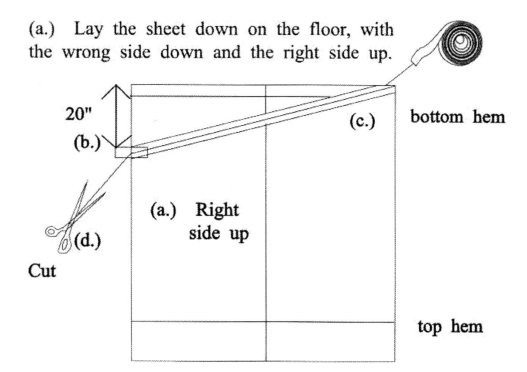

(b.) Measure 20" down from the left upper corner of the sheet, and mark with a piece of masking tape, place a strip of tape half on the sheet, and the other half of the tape onto the floor. Use 2" masking tape.

(c.) With another piece of tape, pull off along strip of tape, and start by placing the tape just above the tape marked for the 20". Pull the tape across in a straight line to the far right upper corner of the sheet. Press the tape down to the sheet.

(d.) Cut the sheet along this tape line, by cutting down the middle of the tape. The tape double functions as a guide line as well as keeping the cut ends from fraying.

To make a lined drapery panel follow these directions in addition to the following pages.

No Sew Lined Drapery Panel

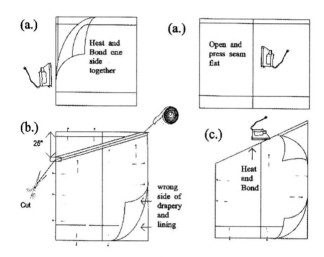

If you want to do an easy, no sew lined drapery panel, then for each panel, use 2 ivory or white colored twin sheets as the lining panel,

(a.) Heat and Bond them together as done on the single drapery side of the twins sheets.

(b.) Place wrong sides of the drapery panel and lining panel together, use straight pins to hold the two panels together, and treat as one panel. Cut on the diagonal as shown with the single sheet, but cut through both layers of the lining and drapery panels.

(c.) After the diagonal cut has been made, use heat and bond to connect the two panels together, at the top diagonal cut and proceed as if it were a single layer panel. OR......

No Sew Lined Drapery Panel

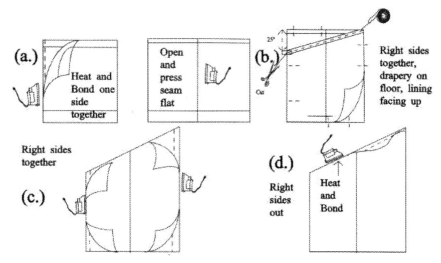

Another no sew option, to make lined drapery panels, for each panel,

(a.) Take 2 ivory or white sheets Heat and Bonded together (or 1 king sheet).
(b.) Pin the lining and drapery panels with right sides together. Place the drapery panel wrong side down on the floor, and the lining panel wrong side facing up. Make the diagonal cut.
(c.) At this time Heat and bond only the sides together. Then turn right sides out, and iron seams flat to the lining side. After ironing seams flat,
(d.) then apply Heat and Bond along the diagonal cut, between the lining and drapery panel. Proceed as though the panel were a single layer panel.

While working with right sides together, keep the drapery panel wrong side down on the floor, and the lining panel wrong side up, so when you turn right sides out, it will be on the same side of the curtain on which you had first thought you had started working.

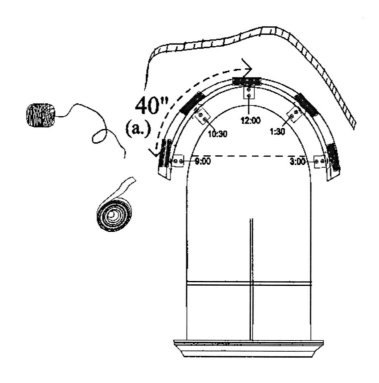

(a.) Measure from the top at 12:00 along the arch down to point measured just above the 9:00 o'clock position. Example: this measurement is 40". To obtain an accurate measurement, use masking tape, masking tape and a string, or use a cloth tape measure.

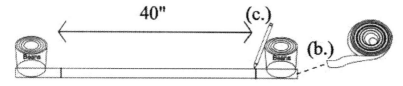

(b.) Using this measurement take a strip of 2" wide masking tape several inches longer, about 45" to 50" long, and with the sticky side up, lay the tape on the floor. You may have to turn the ends of the tape under and stick them down to the floor, to do this.

(c.) Take a heavy object, such as cans of food or such, and with the cans and a pen mark off 40", place the heavy objects on the outside of the marks.

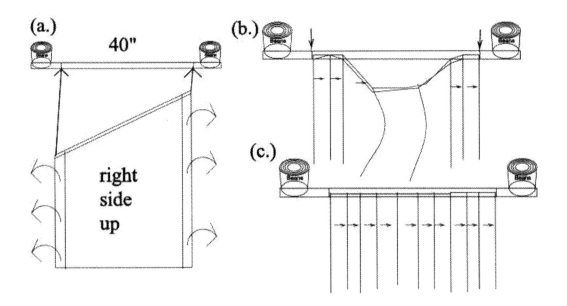

(a.) Place the sheet wrong side down, and right side up, fan fold it along the tape line, between the two marks on the tape. The tape will make it easier to fan fold. Turn the selvage edges under two times, for the folds on both the right and the left sides of the sheet, so the sheet's selvage edges won't show.

(b.) Place the double folded edges of the sheet at the right and left marks on the tape. Start at the edges and work toward the middle, make folds lay to the right.

(c.) For the left side of the curtain, press and make folds to the right. This will create full folds when the curtain is hung in place, as gravity will pull the folds open. Press folds onto the lower 2/3 of the tape. Try and keep the folded pleats smooth and even, press firmly securing them to the tape on the floor.

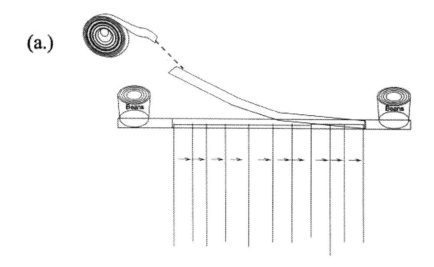

(a.) When finished take another 45" to 50" strip of 2" wide masking tape, this time sticky side down, carefully sandwich the folded pleats between the two strips of tape.

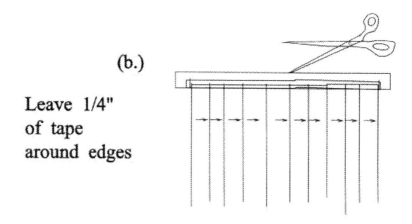

(b.) Press together firmly, trim the excess tape but leave 1/4" of tape around the edges.

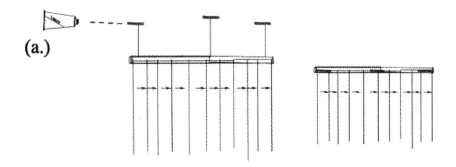

(a.) On the top wrong side of the panel apply the velcro to the tape using velcro adhesive or contact cement for extra needed adhesion. The velcro adhesive or contact cement works better on the masking tape than hot glue or fabric glue.

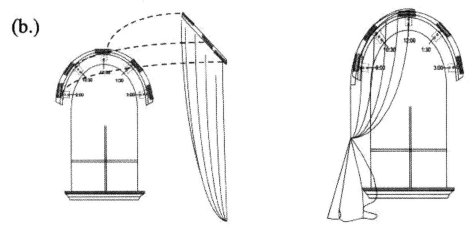

(b.) Marry the velcro of the panel to the velcro at the back of the P.M.M. Board* on the left side.

Repeat the same procedure for the right drapery panel except, remember to do everything in the opposite direction. Place the sheet wrong side down. This time measure, place the tape, and cut from the right side, also press the pleated folds to the left side, this will help gravity to keep the folds open and full.

Bring panel fabric over to cover the exposed P.M.M. Board*. Secure with velcro and or thumbtacks.

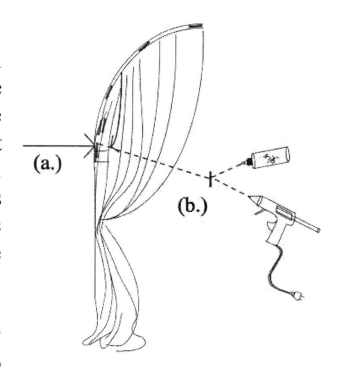

(a.) There will be a small space on the side of the P.M.M. Board*, where the panels may not cover the P.M.M. board*. To correct this bring the panel fabric over to cover the exposed P.M.M Board*.

(b.) Secure with velcro, by applying married up velcro, (female and male velcro married up) on the wrong side of the drapery panels, along the turned under selvage edge. Smooth the drapery panel down along the side of the P.M.M. Board*, allowing the adhesive side of the married up velcro to attach to the P.M.M. Board*. Stand back and evaluate how the curtain hangs, when satisfied then apply hot glue or fabric glue to the velcro for extra adhesion. "Spot weld" velcro with hot glue or fabric glue, to any spots as nccdcd, until the panels flow evenly down the side of the P.M.M. Board*.

Covered Jute Webbing

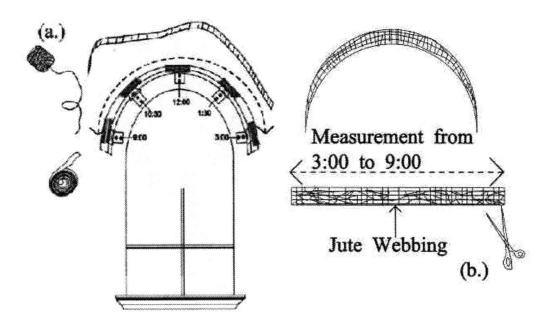

(a.) To make the top, to cover the velcro and tape, measure across the P.M.M. Board* from 3:00 to 9:00 o'clock.

(b.) Cut the Jute webbing this length.

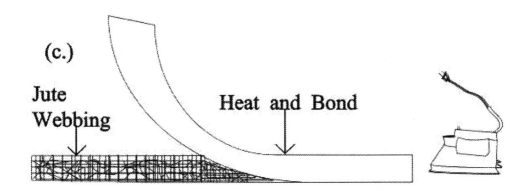

(c.) Iron strips of Heat and Bond to the Jute webbing. Use the Heat and Bond that comes off the bolt, cut strips to fit the Jute Webbing, and iron it onto the Jute webbing.

Jute Webbing with Heat and Bond

(a.)

(a.) If the 1 /2" x 3 1 /4" P.M.M. Board* was used then the 3" Jute Webbing will be fine. (a.) However if the P.M.M. Board used is the 1/2" x 2 7/16" the Jute Webbing will need to be trimmed to fit the board. Trim both, the Jute webbing with the ironed on Heat and Bond, to the size of the width of the P.M.M. Board*. Trimming after the Heat and Bond has been applied causes less fraying of the Jute webbing. Use a sewing gauge and masking tape as a guide

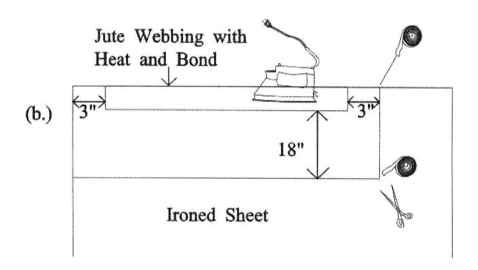

(b.) With an ironed sheet, iron the Heat and bonded Jute webbing to the sheet, side ways along the Jute webbing, 3" from the one end. If there is too much material off the end of the Jute webbing, then use masking tape as a cutting guide and trim within 3" of the Jute webbing, and about 18" down.

(a.) Carefully fold the Jute Webbing over, smooth the fabric and iron flat. Ensure the Jute Webbing and the fabric are even.

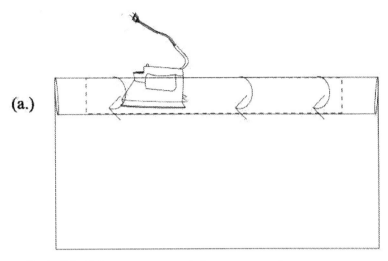

(b.) Fold over and iron again.

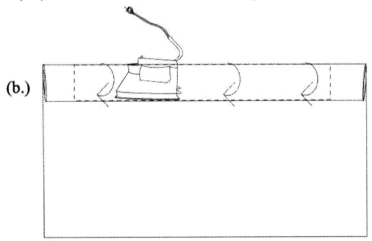

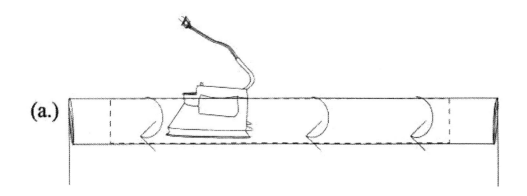

(a.) Fold and iron again for the 3rd time, if you want extra thickness in the covered Jute webbing, other wise folding and ironing twice will be fine.

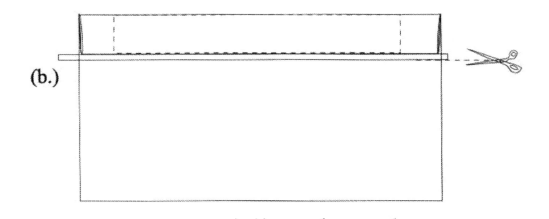

(b.) Cording is optional, if you do not choose to use the cording, then your top cover is just about finished. Run a long strip of tape to use as a cutting guide. Place the tape lengthwise at the bottom of the last fold. Cut along the outside edge of the tape.

(a.)

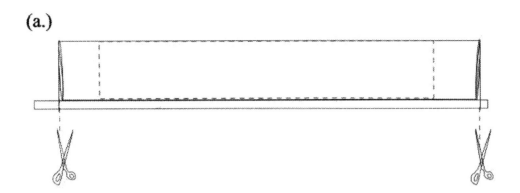

(a.) Leave the tape in place after cutting along the tape's outer edge. Trim edges of tape even with fabric.

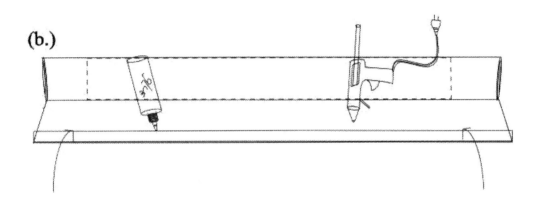

(b.) Turn the taped edge towards the inside to create a fold, the inside edge of the tape should be in the fold, and this fold should be even with the other folds, if not, adjust to make it so. Tack down the taped edge with Heat and Bond, hot glue, or fabric glue.

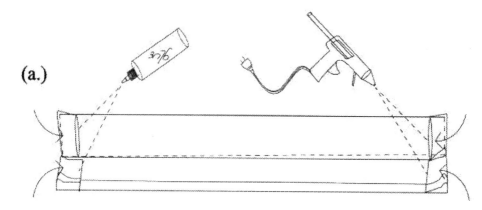

(a.) Turn the side edges in up to the Jute webbing. Be sure corners are neat, and the cover of the Jute webbing is smooth and even. Tack down corners with Heat and Bond, hot glue, or fabric glue.

If you are making the Covered Jute Webbing without the decorative cording then continue. If you are making it with the decorative cording, then stop here and turn to page 74.

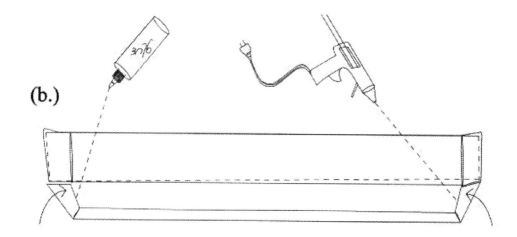

(b.) Make a diagonal fold on the outside bottom corner similar to a hospital corner. Tack this down as well, with either Heat and Bond, hot glue, or fabric glue.

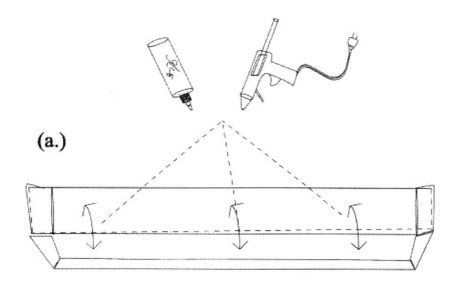

(a.) Fold together and tack down with Heat and Bond, hot glue, or fabric glue. The fabric glue and the Heat and Bond are the most forgiving, if any readjustments are needed. Make sure the covered Jute webbing is smooth and even.

The covered Jute webbing is finished on all edges, however the side with the double fold will be at the back of the P.M.M. Board*, and the single folded edge will face the front of the drapery treatment.

The following section addresses the covered Jute webbing with the decorative cording used. Both the covered Jute webbing with, and without the cording will be applied to the P.M.M. Board* in the same general manner.

(a.)

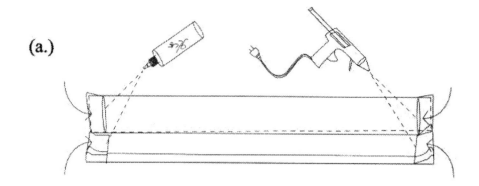

(a.) If you choose to use the decorative cording, then follow the same procedure, as was used for the covered Jute webbing without the cording, up to this point.

Turn the side edges in up to the Jute webbing. Be sure corners are neat, and the cover of the Jute webbing is smooth and even. Tack the corners down with the Heat and bond, hot glue, or fabric glue.

The cording will be sandwiched in between the double fold of the Covered Jute Webbing and the will face the front of the drapery treatment.

(b.) When cutting the decorative cording use clear scotch tape to wrap around the ends to prevent them from fraying, then cut the tape in half so there is only a small amount of tape left on the cording.

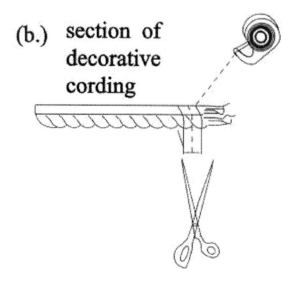

(b.) section of decorative cording

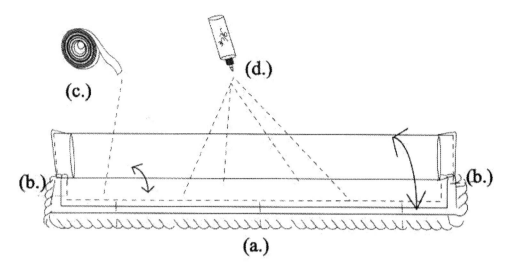

(a.) Wrap the cording around the perimeter of the edge of the covered Jute webbing, with the decorative cording facing out.

(b.) Tuck the ends of the cording in the fold of the middle of the Jute webbing.

(c.) Use masking tape and straight pins to position and hold the decorative cording in place, while you secure it with fabric glue. Wait to cut the end of the cording, until 99% of it has been glued in place, that way you will be sure not to come up too short.

Fabric glue is much more forgiving than hot glue, incase readjustments are needed. First apply the cording to only one side of the folds, then allow for it to dry.

(d.) After the one side has dried then apply the fabric glue to the middle, and finish sandwiching the cording between the two folds. Apply fabric glue to the other side of the cording, so that both of the folds will encase the webb, of the decorative cording.

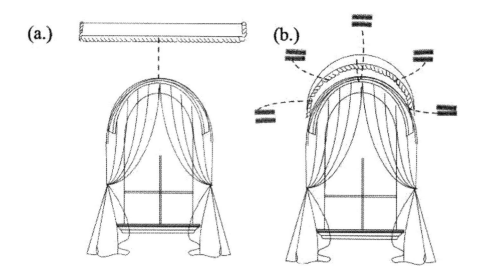

(a.) Lay the covered Jute webbing on top of the pleat folded drapes with the cording facing out. Arrange it so the smoothest and prettiest side is up. More than likely this will be the side with the most padding on top of the Jute webbing.

(b.) To help obtain symmetry of the covered Jute webbing, measure the distance from each end of the P.M.M. Board* that the covered Jute webbing hangs. Once you are certain of the symmetry, then take 10 to 14 strips of velcro 4" to 6" long, married up (female and male married up together). Starting at the center, 12:00 o'clock, slip the married pieces of velcro, between the covered Jute webbing and the top of the pleated drapes. Place one strip at the middle and one to the back at each of the clock positions. Place extra married up velcro at the very ends and any other places needed. Press firmly so each of the sticky sides will hold.

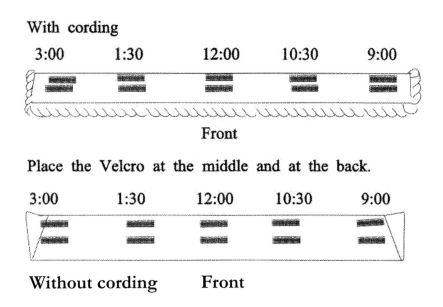

Another way to achieve the same task, is to apply the married up pieces of velcro directly to the covered Jute Webbing.

Find the exact center of the finished covered Jute Webbing by measuring end to end to the nearest 1/8" and divide by 2. Place the first two strips of velcro at the center, 12:00 o'clock, then using the arched P.M.M. Board* measurements obtained earlier when making the drapery panels, roughly estimate the 10:30, 1:30, 3:00, and 9:00 o'clock positions. Place the two strips of velcro at each of the clock positions and at the very ends if needed. Place one strip at the middle and one at the back of the Covered Jute Webbing.

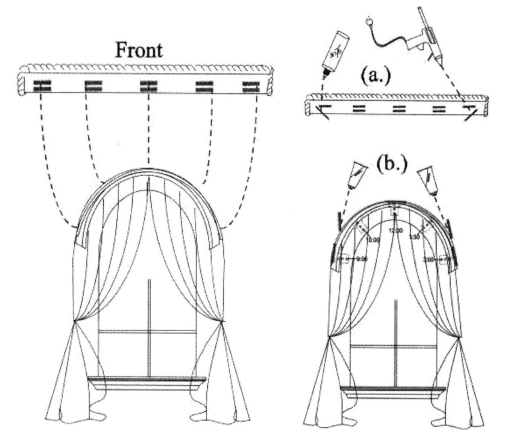

After the positions of the velcro have been established, then stand back and check for symmetry. Once you are satisfied with how they look, then go back and apply fabric glue, hot glue, or velcro adhesive in the tube under the velcro to provide extra adhesion.

(a.) Use the hot glue or fabric glue to glue to the velcro of the Covered Jute Webbing.

(b.) Use the velcro adhesive or contact cement to glue the velcro to the masking tape, wait 24 hours for it to dry.

The following pages show the substitution for the Covered Jute Webbing, the Simply Covered Crinoline. Turn to page 85 for how to finish the window treatment with tie backs.

Simply Covered Crinoline

Check List For Tools and Supplies

* 3" wide Drapery Crinoline length = to cover swags or 3" to 8" past 3:00 and 9:00
* Drapery fabric
* Heat and Bond by the yard, amount to cover the crinoline x 4
* Velcro 10'
* Sissors
* Tape measure
* Iron
* Hot glue gun
* Fabric glue

The Simply Covered Crinoline is an alternative to the Covered Jute Webbing and can be used as a cover in any of the drapery applications where a cover is needed. Here it is shown as a cover to the "Outside Mount Triple Swag".

If making the cover The Simply Covered Crinoline to cover swags then measure and cut the length for the Crinoline after the swags have been mounted so they will be adequately covered.

(a.) To make the Simply Covered Crinoline, use the 3" wide crinoline and cut it to the length of the Swag Lattice, so it will cover all of the swags. If it is used for other drapery treatments then cut it 3" past the 3:00 and 9:00 o'clock positions of the P.M.M. Board*.

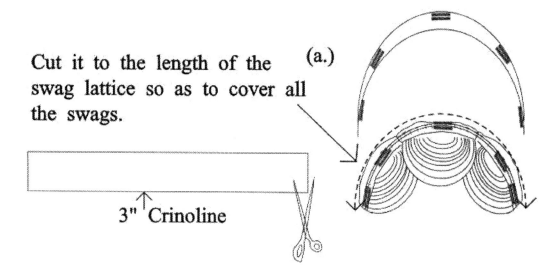

(b.) If the 1/2" x 3 1/4" P.M.M. Board* was used then the 3" Crinoline will be fine, however if the 1/2" x 2 7/16" P.M.M. Board* was used then the Crinoline will need to be trimmed to the width of the P.M.M. Board*. Use a sewing gauge and masking tape as a guide.

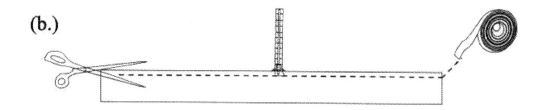

(a.) Cut the drapery fabric length to be 2" longer than the crinoline. Cut the width to be double, plus 1", whatever the width was cut for the crinoline, so there will be enough to completely cover the crinoline and have an inch to overlap.

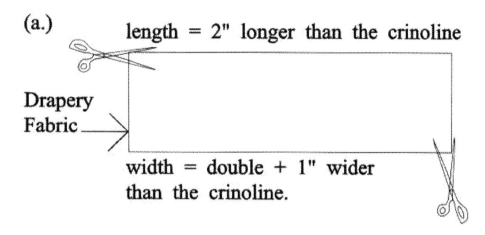

(b.) Use the heat and bond by the bolt, cut strips to fit one side of the crinoline and heat and bond the strips to the one side of the crinoline.

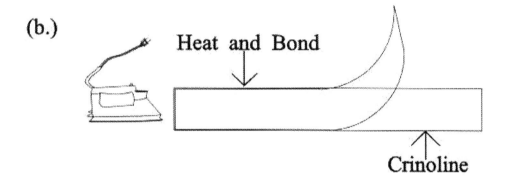

(a.) Place the heat and bonded side of the crinoline down in the middle of the wrong side of the drapery fabric. Be sure to leave a 1" excess of drapery fabric at each end. Heat and bond the crinoline to the wrong side of the drapery fabric.

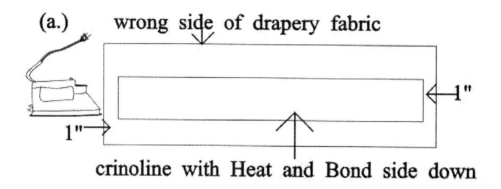

(b.) Fold each of the ends over 1".

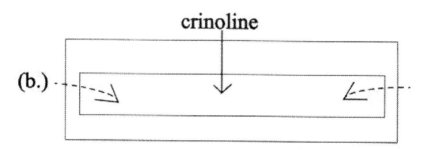

(c.) Cut strips of heat and bond for the ends and heat and bond them down flat.

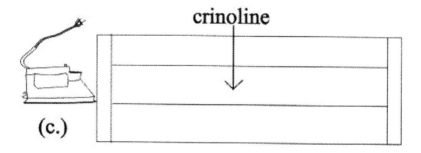

(a.) Cut and apply strips of Heat and Bond to fit each of the sides of the wrong side of the drapery fabric. These will be folded over and Heat and Bonded to the crinoline.

(a.) Apply Heat and Bond on each side of the crinoline.

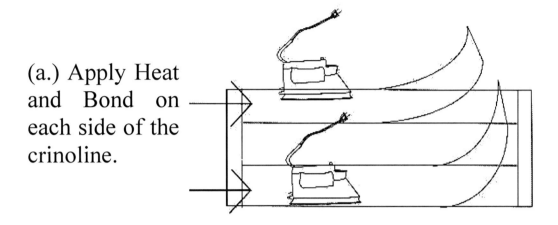

(b.) Fold over one side and Heat and Bond it down, and then fold and overlap the other side, and Heat and Bond it down as well.

(b.)

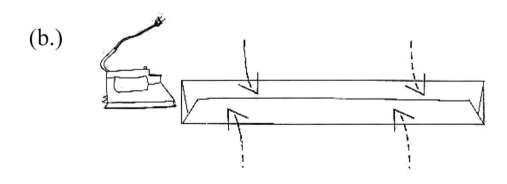

The Simply Covered Crinoline will be applied to the swags and other drapery treatments generally the same as the Covered Jute Webbing. See pages 76 to 78 and follow the same basic instructions. Below is a quick overview.

(a.) Place married up strips of velcro at the middle and the back of the Simply Covered Crinoline, at the clock positions and at the very ends if needed.

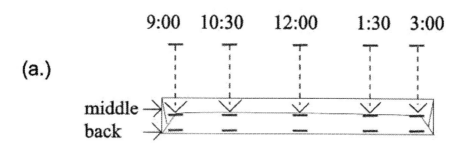

(b.) Place the Simply Covered Crinoline with the married up velcro on top of the swag lattice (or other drapery treatment).

(c.) Once certain of symmetry and how it lays then go back and reinforce with hot glue or fabric glue. Apply extra velcro as needed to secure the Simply Covered Crinoline.

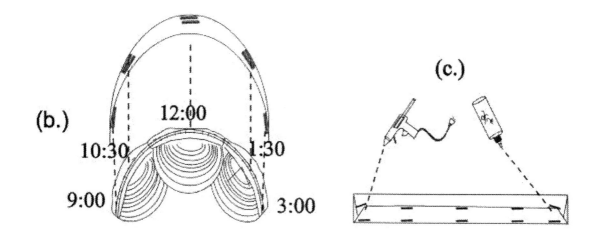

(a.) To encourage distinct folds in the drapery panel, fan fold the panel with a "sideways U" bent finger formation to make folds go in and out. Wrap scrap pieces of fabric around the folds, to hold them in place. Place them at the top, middle, and bottom of the drapery panel. Allow to stand for 2 to 3 days.

(b.) After removing the scrap pieces of fabric utilized to hold the folds, use a steam iron to remove wrinkles and make the folds smooth. Apply tie backs for a finished and polished look. Stand back and evaluate for symmetry and fullness, fluff and puff as needed.

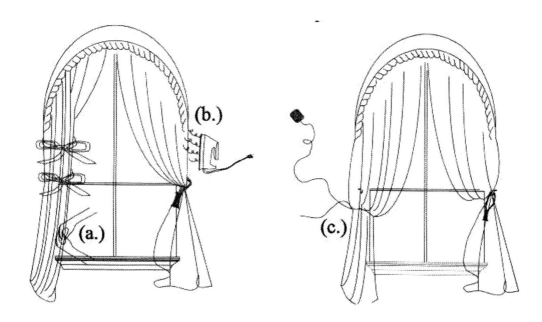

(c.) For a bishop sleeve go a few inches further down, on the drapery panel than you desire the curtain to hang. Tie a string around the drapes several times and tie a knot. Bring the knotted string up to the cup hook or nail and puff the sleeves to look billowy and hide the string. Puddle the bottom on the floor. Add tasseled tie backs for a polished look.

Piecing Together Technique with Bishop Sleeves

If your windows are tall and your drapery treatment needs more length than the length of one long twin sheet, then you can piece your drapery treatment together so they will appear to be one long drapery panel. For this drapery treatment a bishop sleeve is needed, the billowy sleeve of the bishop sleeve is used to hide the excess material and the joining ends. To do this follow instructions as already directed in this chapter, this will give you the top half of your drapery panel. To make the bottom half of the curtain to piece together with the top half follow the instructions on the next two pages. For instructions on how to use this piecing together technique for store bought drapery panels turn to page 89.

(a.) To make the bottom half of one drapery panel, iron two twin sheets flat. If the top half of the drapery panels are lined then make the bottom half lined as well except with out the diagonal cut at the top.

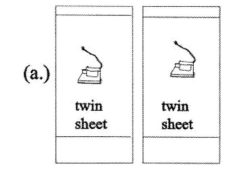

(b.) Turn the selvage edges under twice, and fan fold the panels together side to side, placing bottom hem to bottom hem and top hem to top hem. Placing the wide hem of the sheet at the bottom will avoid having excessive material bunched up in the bishop sleeve from the bottom half of the drapery panel.

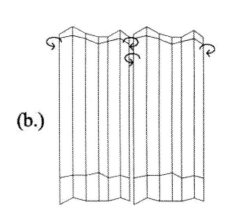

(c.) Either puddle the bottom drapery panel or put in a double 6" hem at the bottom (hang 1/2" to 1" off the floor). Measure from the cuphook to 1 /2" to 1 " from the floor, at this measurement tie the top of the drapery panel with a string ensuring the selvage edges stay turned under as the string is tied into a knot.

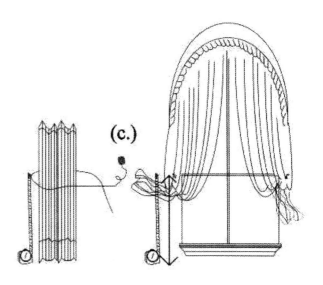

(a.) To make the bishop sleeve out of the top half of the drapery panel go a (a.) few inches further down on the drapery panel than you desire the curtain to hang.

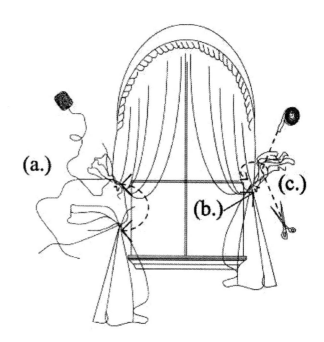

At this point tie a string around the drapes several times, and then tie a knot. Tie the end of the top half and the bottom half of the drapery panels together.

(b.) Use the string that has both the top half and the bottom half tied together and bring this up to hang on the cup hook or nail. Hide the string and the two joining ends in the billow of the bishop sleeve. Add tasseled tie backs for elegance and either hem or puddle the bottom half of the drapery panel on the floor.

(c.) If you have an abundance of material when joining the two cnds then after you have made all the adjustments arranging the two ends together, then go back and trim the ends to make hiding them in the billow of the bishop sleeve more manageable. Use masking tape as a cutting guide, and to keep the frayed ends from unraveling.

No Sew Customized Store Bought Drapes

This same piecing together technique can be used to make store bought drapes appear custom made for your arched window treatment.

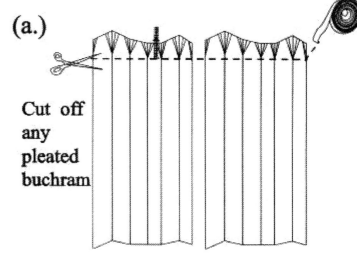

(a.) Some of the store bought drapes have a pleated buckram at the top, if so then cut this off, use masking tape and a sewing gauge as a guide.

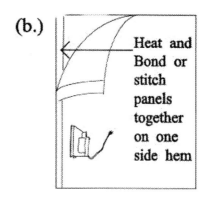

(b.) With right side together, Heat and bond two drapery panels together at their side hem on one side.

(c.) Open and press seem flat. Follow the basic instructions in this chapter including the piecing together technique on page 88, substituting one store bought drapery panel to be the equivalent of one twin sheet.

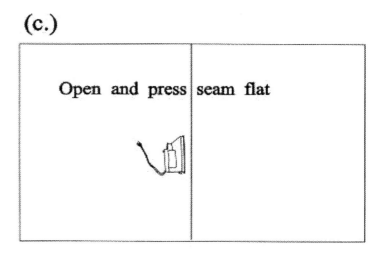

This window treatment can be very economical, especially if coordinating sheets can be found in large area outlet malls, discount stores or white sales. In a bedroom, the use of sheets allows for a relatively inexpensive way to coordinate the design of the window treatments with bed linens.

Use tassel or fabric tie backs for added elegance. For fabric tie backs turn to page 112.

For privacy add miniblinds, and or sheers.

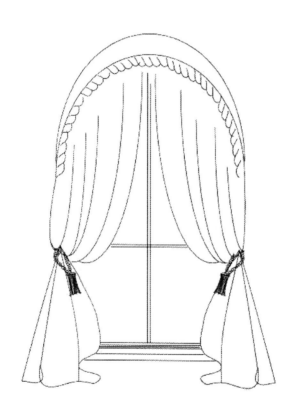

Chapter 5
Rod Pocket Sleeve Drapery Panels With A Diagonal Cut To Fit Arched Windows

The rod pocket sleeve can be used as the basic under drapery panel treatment for swags and top treatments. The tie backs can be store bought tassel tie backs or a fabric tie back can be made from the drapery and lining fabric along with a stiff material. See page 112.

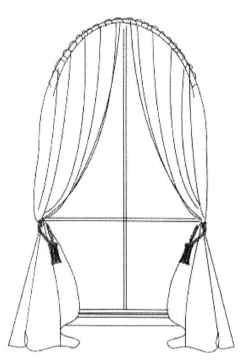

These curtains can either be sew or no sew, and whichever you choose the same basic principles will be used. You will first need to make the drapery panels and finish the side hems.

The following pages will give some basic ideas for making lined drapery panels, then to customize them to fit arched windows.

* Polystyrene Lattice Strip abbreviated as P.L. Strip*
* Polystyrene Moulding Mounting Board abbreviated as P.M.M. Board*

Check List for Tools and Supplies

* Drapery fabric
* Drapery lining
* Matching thread
* For No Sew
  1 roll of 3/4"
  Heat and Bond
* Short thumbtacks
* Masking tape
* Velcro
* 2 Tassle tie back
  holders or
* For fabric tie backs
  see page 112
* Sissors
* Iron
* P.L. Strip*
* Hot glue
* Fabric glue
* Tape measure
* Dissappearing ink pen or Dressmakers chalk
* 2 Cup hooks or nails
* Steam iron

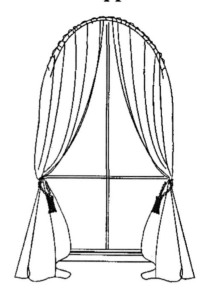

The following page gives instructions for drapery and lining fabric yardage estimations. It is helpful to have the P.M.M. Board* already mounted to get a more accurate yardage estimation, however you can estimate by measuring from where you think the P.M.M. Board* will be mounted and add an extra yard of fabric per panel. It will be helpful to know which window treatment will be used and how much off the glass the window treatment will hang.

Drapery and Lining Fabric Yardage Estimation

(a.) Measure from top of the arch to the floor, add 36" (for the puddles, rod pocket sleeve, and trim off allowance) then multiply this number by 2 for each, the drapery and lining fabric yardage. This will be for a single width of fabric for each panel. For windows with a width greater than the width of fabric, see the following page.

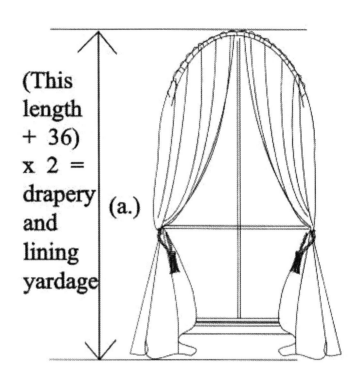

(This length + 36) x 2 = drapery and lining yardage (a.)

To this yardage estimation add the yardage estimation for the swag top treatment, see chapters 7, 8, or 9. For fabric tie backs add an extra 1/4 yard, see page 112.

If you are using a drapery fabric with a large decorative print, then purchase an extra repeat of fabric for each panel and each swag, so the curtains will appear even. Start each panel and swag at the beginning or the same place in the repeat.

To get the "yardage" figure, divide the number of inches by 36, and round up to the next 1/4 of a yard to know what to tell your fabric store sales person.

The general rule of thumb for the fullness of a gathered window treatment is for the fabric to be 2 1/2 to 3 times the window width.

(a.) If the width of the window is much greater than the width of the drapery fabric then for each panel either

(b.) split a width of the fabric or

(c.) for a fuller look and ease add another width of fabric. If a more open look (with the drapery panels just to the side) is preferred then one width of fabric is likely to be enough.

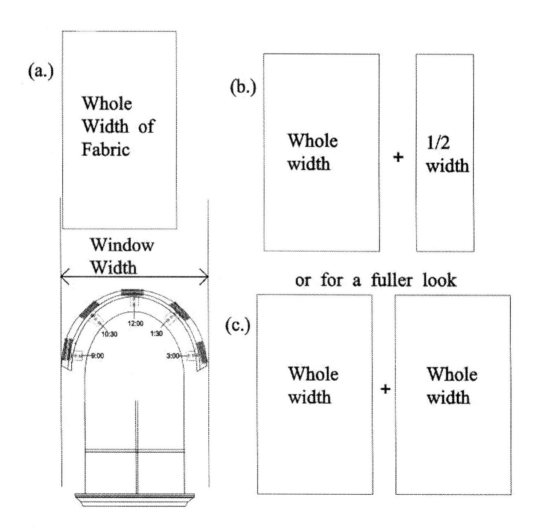

Use the measurements obtained on page 93 to make the drapery panels. For each of the drapery panels, cut the drapery and lining fabric length, the length of the measurement from the top of the arch to the floor plus 32".

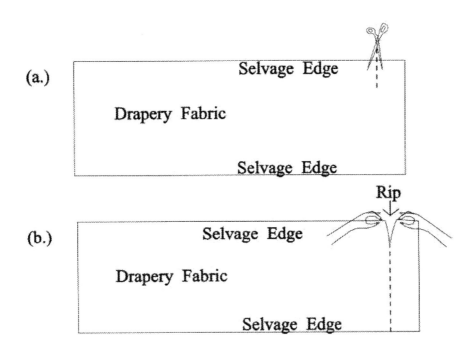

To cut the fabric test a small piece of the fabric, if the drapery fabric rips easily without pulling out of shape, then rip the fabric so it will tear along a straight line. This is the easiest way to obtain an even straight edge. If the fabric pulls out of shape do not rip it, see the next page.

(a.) First make a small cut with scissors on one selvage edge.

(b.) Then rip smartly, the material should tear evenly, as evidenced by being able to pull a single strand of thread from selvage edge to selvage edge.

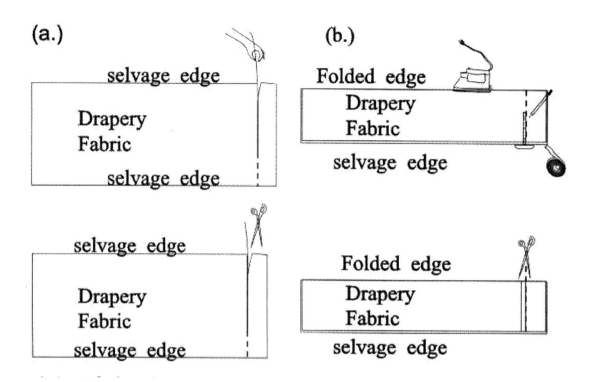

(a.) If the drapery fabric pulls out of shape and gets cattywompas when you rip it, then you will need to do it the harder way by pulling a thread and cut along the line created by the pulled thread, to get a perfectly straight edge.

(b.) You can achieve a roughly straight edge by using a T-square and a strip of masking tape as a cutting guide. Fold the material in half from selvage edge to selvage edge, ensure evenous and then iron the folded side. Line up the T-square to the selvage edge and use masking tape, invisible ink pen, or dress makers chalk to make a straight cutting line. Check for evenous with the T-square on both the folded and the selvage edges, and then cut along the cutting line.

Directions For Lined Drapery Panels

As with a lined skirt, a drapery panel will look and hang better being lined. Additionally a lined drapery panel will give more body to your curtains and a less expensive drapery fabric can be used. There are a couple of ways in which to make a lined drapery panel.

To cut the drapery lining, either use the T-square method or use the straight cut edge of the drapery fabric to cut the drapery lining. This is because often the lining does not stay true to the pulled string or rip method.

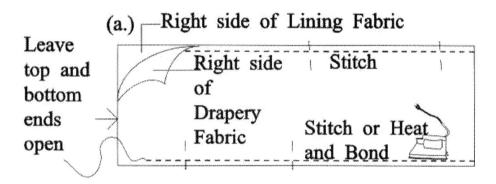

(a.) One way to make a lined drapery panel is if the drapery fabric and the drapery lining are the same width. Place the drapery panel and the lining panel right sides together, pin, and then sew a 5/8" seam allowance along both sides of the panel being sure to include the selvage edges, leave the top and bottom of the drapery panel open at this time. If the no sew method is preferred, use Heat and Bond in place of stitching.

(a.) Iron the seams open and flat, then turn the panel right side out through the opening at the top or bottom. Iron the panel flat with the seam to the lining side.

(a.)

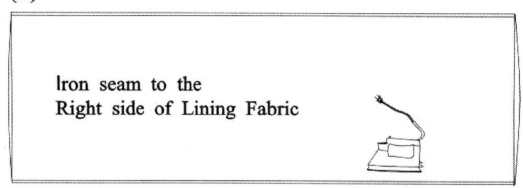

(b.) Then iron the panel flat, ironing from the middle out to the sides. Use a pillowcase or pressing cloth when ironing the drapery fabric so to be sure not to scorch the fabric.

(b.)

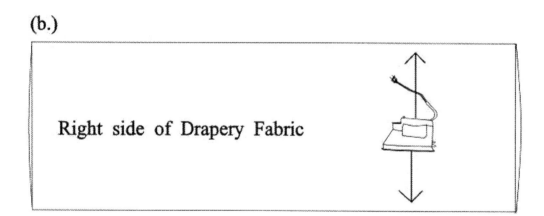

(a.) The other common way drapery panels are lined, when the drapery fabric and the drapery lining are the same width, is to cut the width of the drapery lining 2" to 3" on each side, so as to have a double 1 " to 1 1 /2" side hem, respectively.

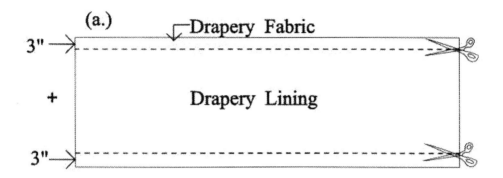

(b.) The easier way to accomplish this same effect is to buy the drapery lining 6" less in width than the drapery material Many drapery fabrics come in a 54" width, and drapery linings in a 48" width can easily be found. This affords the drapery panel a generous double 1 1 /2" side hem without a lot of unnecessary fussing and cutting.

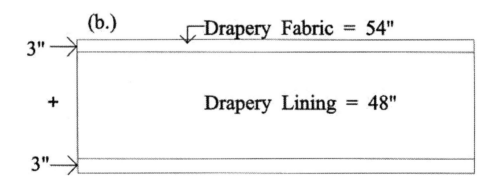

(a.) Pair the drapery lining and the drapery fabric wrong sides together. Use a sewing gauge to center the lining in the middle of the drapery fabric and pin them together.

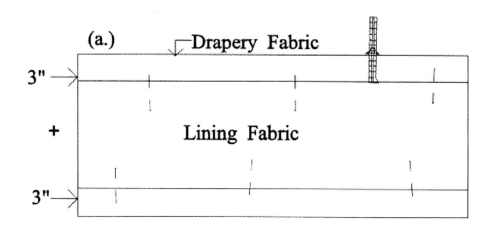

(b.) Working from the lining side of the panel, Fold the drapery selvage edge over 1 1 /2" pin and press, then fold over again another 1 1 /2" pin and press. Whipstitch the double side hem by hand, or use the "Blind Hem Stitch" selector of your sewing machine, or if the no sew method is preferred use the iron on hem binding tape.

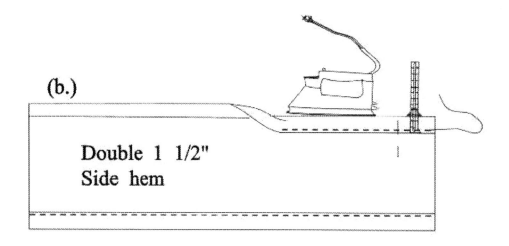

The drapery panel will have a diagonal cut at the top so it can follow the basic curve of the arched window. The angle for the diagonal cut will be determined by the following measurements.

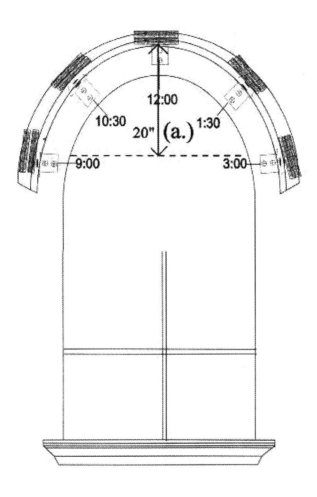

(a.) Measure from the imaginary straight line, just above the 3:00 and 9:00 o'clock position (of the clock analogy), on the half round window. This is where the window first starts to straighten out the curve. Measure to the top highest point of the arch, at 12:00 o'clock. Example: this figure is 20".

Clear a large working space on the floor so there will be enough room to keep the panel even, smooth and flat.

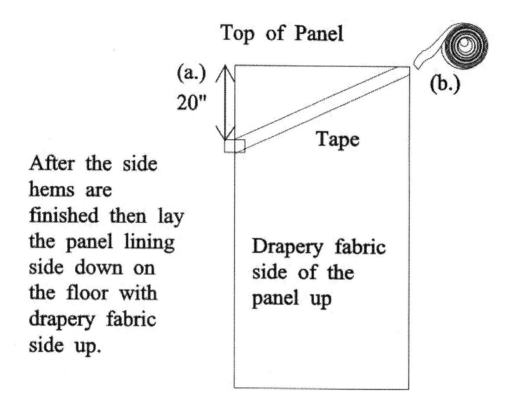

(a.) Using the example measurement obtained on the previous page, measure 20" down from the left upper corner of the panel, and mark this with a piece of masking tape, place a strip of tape half on the panel, and the other half of the tape onto the floor. Use 1 " masking tape.

(b.) With another piece of tape, pull off a long strip of tape, and start by placing the tape just above the tape marked for the 20". Pull the tape across in a straight line to the far right upper corner of the panel. Press the tape down to the panel.

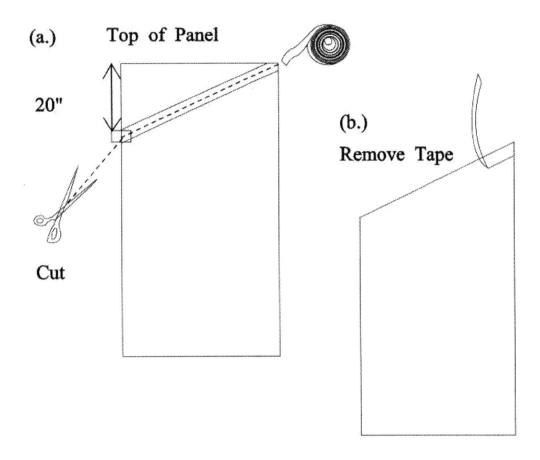

(a.) Cut the panel along this tape line, by cutting down the middle of the tape. The tape functions as a cutting guide line.

(b.) After the diagonal cut has been made then, carefully remove the tape.

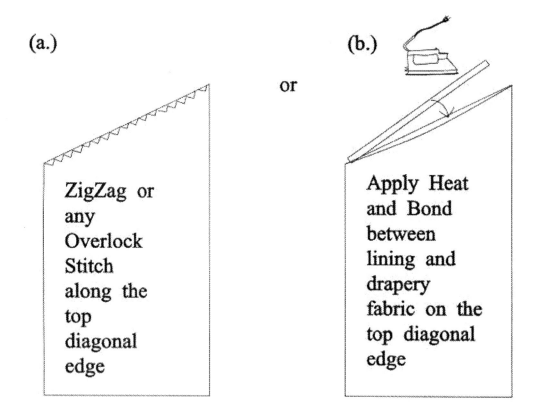

(a.) If you are using the sewing method then run a zigzag stitch or any over locking stitch along the top diagonal edge to prevent unraveling.

(b.) If the no sew method is preferred then apply Heat and Bond to the diagonal cut edge. First slip a strip of 3/4" Heat and Bond in between the lining and drapery fabric, and then fuse them together at the top diagonal edge.

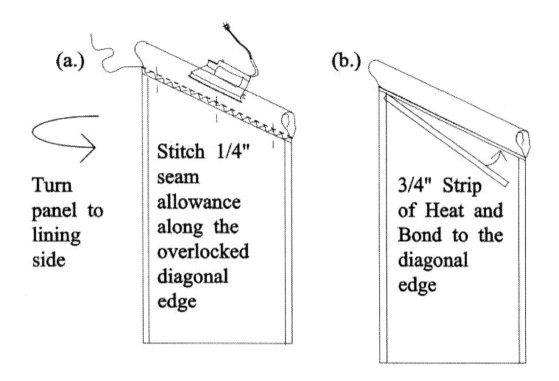

(a.) After turning the panel over to the lining side, fold the top over 2" to the lining side, pin and press. Sew in a rod pocket for the P.L. Strip*. Use a straight stitch and sew along the edge with the overlock stitch leaving a 1 /4 " seam allowance.

(b.) If your are using the no sew method then fold the edge over 2 1 /2" and fuse a strip of 3/4" Heat and Bond to the lining side of the drapery panels. Apply the 3/4" strip along the diagonal edge. Later when the panel is sheered on the P.L. Strip* a few short thumbtacks may be added to the top of the P.L. Strip* to create distinct folds in the rod pocket since the top of the pocket is not attached to the lining in the middle of the panel.

Since the bottom of the drapery panel will puddle on the floor the finish to the ends will not show. The finish to the ends can easily be done in a number of ways:

(a.) Simply pin the ends and run an overlock stitch to the raw ends to prevent them from unraveling.

(b.) Turn the raw edges of each the drapery and lining fabric inward 1 /2" towards the inside of the drapery panel pin, iron and then run a straight stitch along the bottom.

(c.) For the no sew way to finish the ends of the drapery panel, turn the raw edges of each, the lining and drapery fabric in 1 /2" towards the inside of the drapery panel and pin. Iron flat, remove the pins and slip a strip of the Heat and Bond in between them, and bond them together.

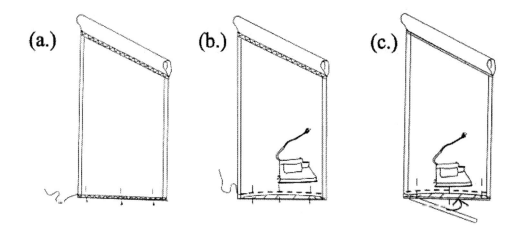

Repeat the same procedure for the right sided panel except the measuring and cutting will be in the reverse. This time measure down from the right side of the panel and place the tape from the measured point on the right side to the upper left hand corner, etc.

(a.) Sheer the panels on the Polystyrene P.L. Strip* where the left panel is on the left, and the right panel is on the right side of the Polystyrene P.L. Strip*.

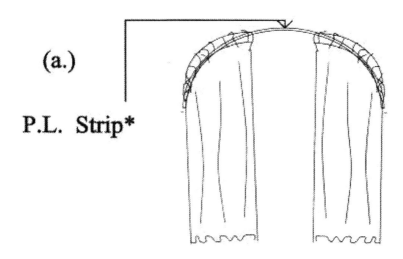

(b.) Find and mark the exact middle of the P.L. Strip* arrange the curtains so that they meet at 12:00 o'clock, and that the rod pocket ends 2" to 3" above 3:00 and 9:00 o'clock, use thumbtacks to hold them in place.

(c.) If a more open look to the drapery treatment is preferred, leave the panels open in the middle. Place the panels evenly spaced from the exact center, 12:00 o'clock, use thumbtacks to hold them in place.

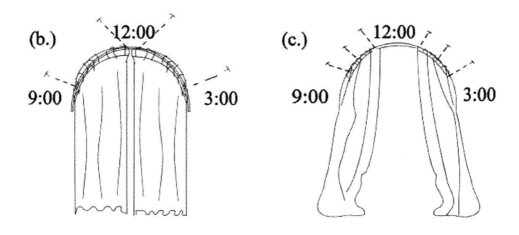

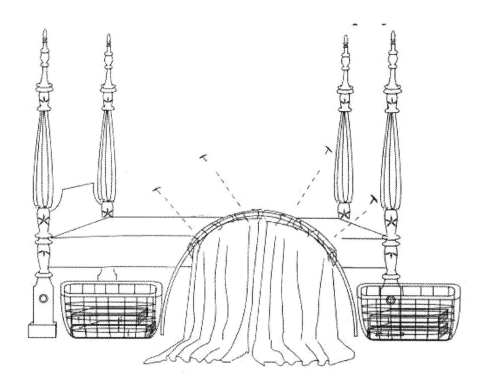

A good place to work with your P.L. Strip* and drapery panel is next to a bed or table where you can lean the P.L. Strip* so it will stand upright in a curved form position. Use 2 objects to keep the ends of the P.L. Strip* from slipping away. One example could be 2 laundry baskets with clothes or books in them for weight. Approximate the width of the window and place the laundry baskets that far apart next to the bed or table. Bend the P.L. Strip* so each end rests on the carpet against the laundry baskets. Let the P.L. Strip* lean against the bed or table. This will keep it in an upright position. You will need to work with the P.L. Strip* bent in the upright position because in this position you can approximate the curve of your window. If you try and work with the P.L. Strip* flat all the time it will be harder to see how the curtain is likely to hang.

Thumbtack, hot glue, or use fabric glue to apply strips of velcro to the underside of the sheered up drapery panel and the underside of the P.L. Strip*. Apply them at the 12:00, 1:30, 10:30, 3:00, and 9:00 o'clock positions, and also at the very ends of the P.L. Strip* if necessary, so as to marry to velcro in coordinating positions on the front edge of the P.M.M. Board*.

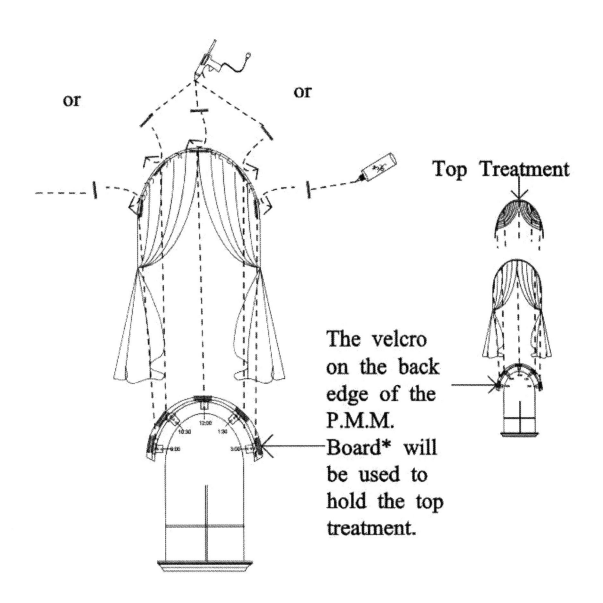

Top Treatment

The velcro on the back edge of the P.M.M. Board* will be used to hold the top treatment.

Since the under drapery panels are in front of the top treatment, there will be a small space left showing the top treatment's P.L. Strip* and the P.M.M. Board*.

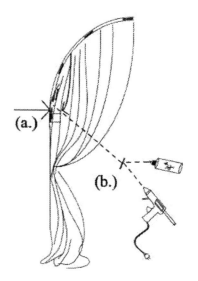

(a.) To correct this apply small strips of married up velcro or thumbtacks to the edge of the drapery panel to the P.L. Strip* of the top treatment.

(b.) Place the velcro on the wrong side of the drapery panel along the side hem line. Start placing the marrying velcro up under the top treatment and continue as needed until the panel flows down the side of the P.M.M. Board* evenly. Spot weld marrying velcro or thumbtack any spots as needed.

(c.) To secure the very end of the P.L. Strip* to the end of the P.M.M. Board*, slip a strip of 1" masking tape up in the small gap between the wall and the P.M.M. Board*. Wrap the tape completely around the two ends. Here it is shown illustrated without the drapery treatment, but do this after the drapery treatment has been applied.

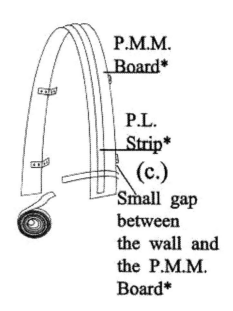

110

Allow the bottom of the panels to luxuriously puddle on the floor with a finish to the raw edges as described on page 106. Or if preferred stitch in a conventional double bottom hem, or for the no sew method use iron on hem binding tape.

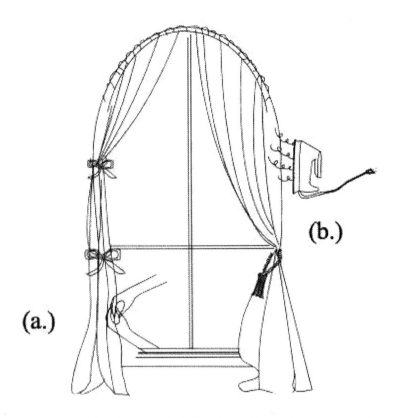

(a.) To encourage distinct folds in the drapery panel, fan fold the panel with a "sideways U" bent finger formation to make folds go in and out. Wrap scrap pieces of fabric around the folds, to hold them in place. Place them at the top, middle, and bottom of the drapery panel. Allow to stand for 2 to 3 days.

(b.) After removing the scrap pieces of fabric utilized to hold the folds, use a steam iron to remove wrinkles and make the folds smooth. Apply tie backs for a finished and polished look. Stand back and evaluate for symmetry and fullness, fluff and puff as needed.

Fabric Tie Backs

For the tie backs use the store bought tassel tie backs or make your own out of the drapery and lining fabric. A stiff material such as crinoline, drapery header, buchram, (or even fussible craft pellon ironed onto lining fabric) will be used inbetween the drapery and lining fabric.

Cut the stiff material to desired length (recommended 22") and to the desired width if needed (recommended 3" or 4"). Cut the drapery and lining fabric each 1" wider and 1 " longer than the stiff material (1 3/4" for the no sew method).

Place drapery and lining fabric with right sides together and stitch a 3/8" seam allowance on three sides, the two long and one short side. If using the no sew method, use 3/4" Heat and Bond on three sides.

Iron seams open and flat, then turn right sides out and press flat to the lining side. Slip in the stiff material. Turn the open end over 1 /4" twice to the lining side and whipstitch close.

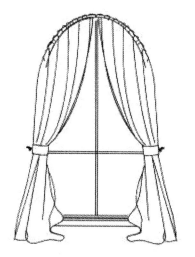

Connect the two ends of the tie back with a small whipstitch, and slip the tie back up from the bottom of the drapery panel. Hold in place with an upholstery nail to the wall or stitch a small plastic ring at the back and hang on a cuphook or nail.

Chapter 6
Two Short Side Boards Drapery Panels

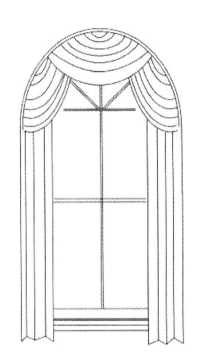

The "Two Short Side Boards Drapery Panels" is a good under drapery panel treatment for the window treatments "Outside Mount Triple Swag" chapter 7, and "Half Dimension Swags" chapter 8. This will be a stationary window treatment, non functional.

The "Two Short Side Boards Drapery Panels" application is also an excellent choice for store bought ready made swags and drapery panels. Furthermore it is a wonderful way to cut down on expense, especially if the drapery fabric is costly. A tall majestic look can be achieved with much less fabric involved, than if the panels were to go up and around the arch.

* Polystyrene Lattice Strip abbreviated as P.L. Strip*
* Polystyrene Moulding Mounting Board abbreviated as P.M.M. Board*

Checklist for Tools and Supplies

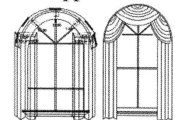

* 1 P.M.M. Board* same size as used for the outside mount
* Metal tape measure
* Velcro
* Hot glue gun
* 1 Package of 4 small corner irons with screws
* Hollow wall anchors (8, optional)
* #8 x 5/8" Phillips flat head screws (8)
* Level
* Hacksaw
* Electric drill
* Pencil
* one P.L. Strip* and masking tape (optional)
* Lead weighted tape yardage = width of fabric x 2
* Thumbtacks
* For No Sew: Heat and Bond, and hem binding tape.
* For Sewing method: Matching thread, (Gathering tape optional)
* Drapery fabric
* Lining fabric
* Steam iron
* Mounted Swag treatments for either Chapter 7 or 8

The following page gives instructions for fabric yardage estimations. It is helpful to have the short side boards already mounted for a more accurate yardage estimation, however you can estimate by measuring from where you think the short side boards will be mounted and purchasing an extra yard per panel to accommodate errors. It will be necessary to have the swags already made and mounted to determine the length of the short side boards.

Drapery and Lining Fabric Yardage Estimation

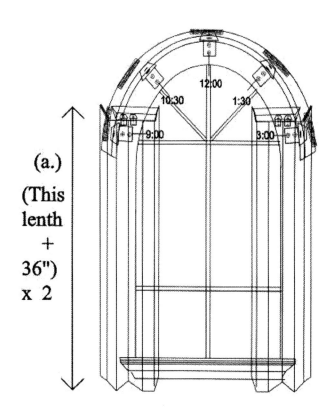

(a.) Measure from the top of the Short Side Board to the floor add 36" (for a 3" top hem and double 6" bottom hem and trim off allowance) then multiply this figure by 2, for each the drapery and lining fabric.

(a.) (This lenth + 36") x 2

To this yardage estimation add the yardage estimation for the swag top treatment, see chapter 7 or 8.

If using a drapery fabric with a large print, then purchase an extra "repeat" of drapery fabric for each panel and swag, so the print will match up. When measuring and cutting the fabric, start cutting for each panel and swag at the same place in the "repeat" of the fabric.

To get the yardage figure, divide the number of inches by 3 6, and round up to the next 1 /4 of a yard to know what to tell your fabric store sales person.

The swag top treatment will need to be mounted first so the length of the short side board can be determined. The length of the short side board can be an individual preference, but generally it's length is the distance between the outer edge of the top treatment to the inner edge of same top treatment minus 2".

(a.) The point at which to take this measurement is just above the 3:00 and 9:00 o'clock positions.

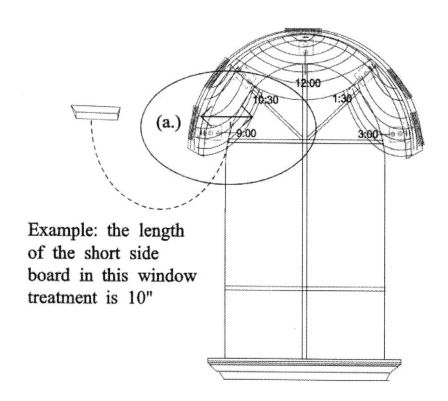

Example: the length of the short side board in this window treatment is 10"

For example, if your top window treatment for a triple swag is 7 inches outside the window's frame, and the swag reaches to 5 inches inside the window, then the short side board should be about 10", (7 + 5 = 12, then 12 - 2 = 10" .)

(a.) To cut the short side board out of the P.M.M. Board* to the desired length, measure then mark across it with a pencil.

(b.) Use a hacksaw, and start cutting on the thin side of the P.M.M. Board* first. It is better for the short side board to be a little too short than to be too long, because it will extend past the inside edge of the top window treatment.

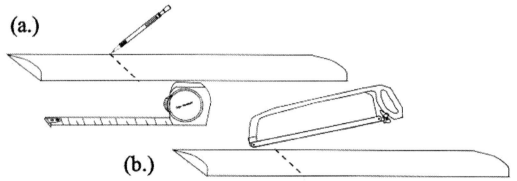

(c.) **After cutting the short side board, check to be sure that it will be completely hidden up underneath the swag.**

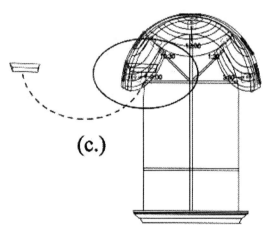

Repeat the same process for the other short side board, that will be for the other side of the window.

(a.) The short side board will need to be placed as close as possible to the inside of the arched P.M.M. Board* so it will not look detached from the swags.

(b.) The outside edge of the short side board's drapery panel will wrap around the top side of the P.M.M. Board*, underneath the top treatment.

(c.) Place the short side board about 2 inches above the 3:00 and 9:00 o'clock positions of the arch, in many of the arched windows this is where the top of the square of the glass aluminum casing begins, and at this point the arch is straightening out.

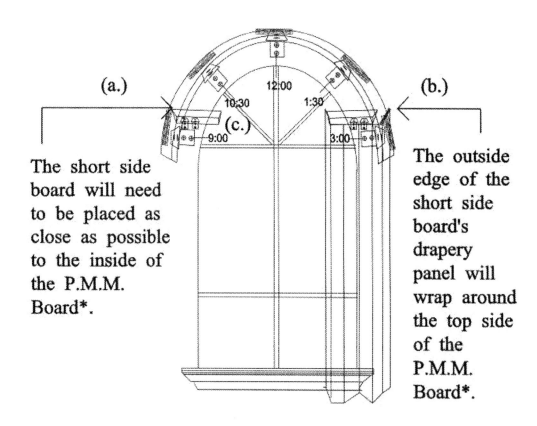

The short side board will need to be placed as close as possible to the inside of the P.M.M. Board*.

The outside edge of the short side board's drapery panel will wrap around the top side of the P.M.M. Board*.

To mount the short side boards, first apply the corner irons to the under side of the short side board. In this instance it is alright to attach the screws and corner irons into the short side board first, rather than attaching the screws and corner irons to the wall first as was done in mounting the P.M.M. Board*, because there will be no bending stress placed on the short side board.

(a.) Keep the wide side of the short side board to the front and the thin side of it next to the wall.

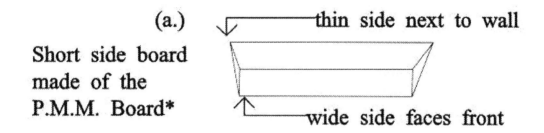

Short side board made of the P.M.M. Board*

(b.) With the #8 x 5/8" flat head phillips screws apply a corner iron to the end of the short side board that will be the closest to the arched mounted P.M.M. Board*, and then apply a second corner iron 2" to 3" in from the first corner iron.

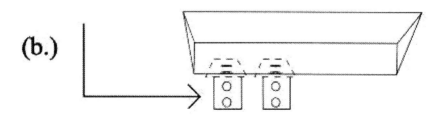

Hold the short side board to the desired position on the wall,

(a.) Use a level to ensure that the short side board is straight, and then mark the wall with a pencil where the holes in the corner irons are.

(b.) Hollow wall anchors are optional, if used then predrill pilot holes in which to place the hollow wall anchors. If they are not used then predrill very small pilot holes for the screws from the package of corner irons.

(c.) If the hollow wall anchors were use then place them in the predrilled holes, and then (d.) screw in the corner irons into the hollow wall anchors or the pilot holes.

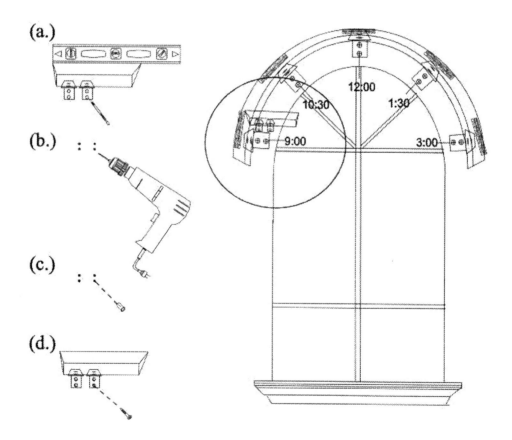

(a.) To place the other short side board, use a "landmark" such as the window sill or if the window has the square aluminum casing below the palladian then this will serve as a good "landmark" or reference point. Measure the distance from the reference point to the top of the short side board.

(b.) Mark this measurement on the other side of the window's frame.

(c.) Place the top of the other short side board at this point and as close as possible to the arched P.M.M. Board*. Use a level to ensure the short side board is straight and proceed as was done for the first short side board.

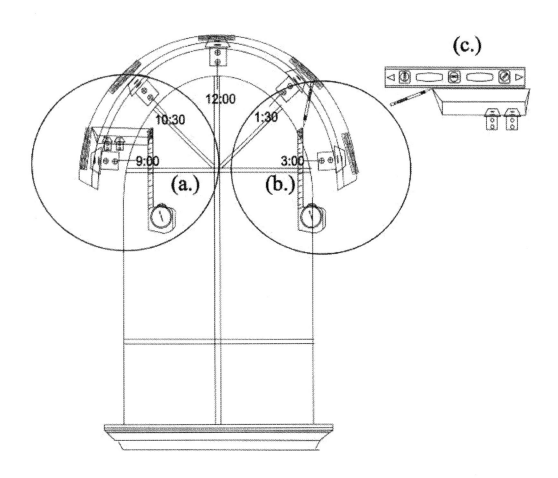

Use a hot glue gun or fabric glue to apply the velcro to the

(a.) front, and to the

(b.) inside edge of the short side board, and then onto the

(c.) top of the P.M.M. Board* in direct line with the short side boards, so the drapery panel will hang down the side of the P.M.M. Board*. Do not apply velcro to the outside edge of the short side board as this side will be as close as possible to the P.M.M. Board*.

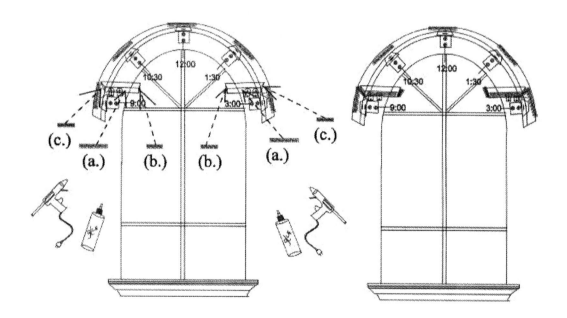

The drapery panels can be applied in a variety of ways. They can be applied to the same length short pieces of P.L. Strip* and then velcroed to the short side board, or the velcro can be applied directly to the drapery panels and married to the short side boards.

Follow any of the basic drapery panel directions as outlined in chapter 5 "Rod Pocket Sleeve Drapery Panels With A Diagonal Cut To Fit Arched Windows", except do not make the diagonal cut at the top. Use the measurements obtained on page 115 to make the drapery panels. For each of the drapery panels, cut the drapery and lining fabric length, the length of the measurement from the top of the short side board to the floor plus 18".

Below are the two basic outlines for drapery panels for a more detailed explanation see the above mentioned chapter. Either of the drapery panels,

(a.) without or

(b.) with a double side hem, will work fine.

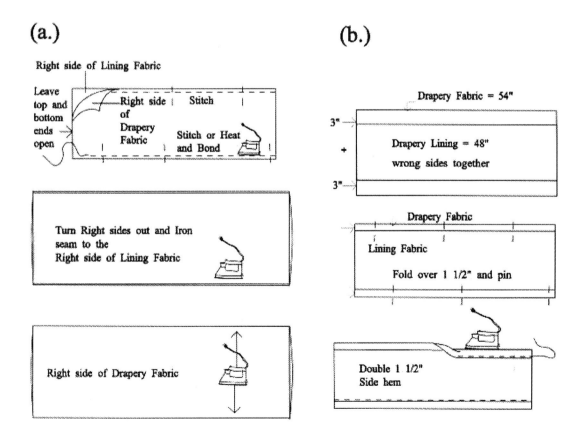

The drapery panels will be attached to the short side boards with velcro. The top of the drapery panel will need to gathered. To gather the top of the panel use any of the following methods, gathering tape, or stitch in a rod pocket sleeve, or pleat the top directly onto a P.L. Strip*. Each will be discussed in turn.

Gathering Tape

To use the gathering tape,

(a.) Turn the top of the drapery panel over 1 1 /2" twice to the lining side, press and then straight stitch a 1 1/2" hem.

(b.) Stitch the gathering tape in place 1 /2" from top.

(c.) Secure one end of the gathering tape and then pull up the gathering tape to the width for the drapery panel to go around the short side board and on top of the P.M.M. Board*, secure the other end of the gathering tape.

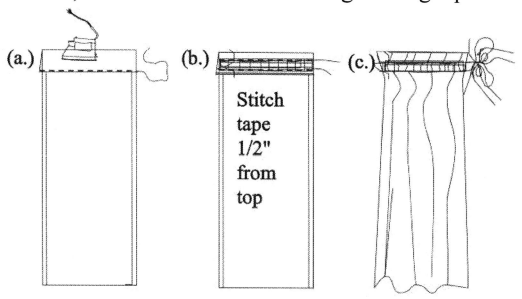

Velcro can be applied to the drapery panel in which the gathering tape was used in a couple of ways.

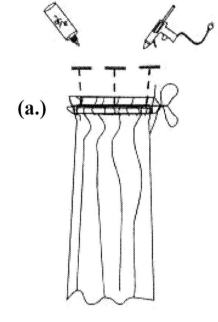

(a.) One is to apply the velcro directly to the back of the drapery panel.

(b.) The other way is to use P.L. Strip*, velcro and thumbtacks. Measure and cut (with gardening shears or the like) the P.L. Strip* into 3 pieces so as to fit each of the sides of the short side boards, the front, the inside, and the side that will go around the P.M.M. Board*. Connect these 3 pieces together with two, 2" strips of 1" masking tape, leave a small space between each of the pieces so they will bend.

3 pieces of P.L. Strip* connected with masking tape

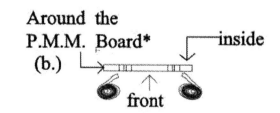

(c.) Place the 3 connected pieces of the P.L. Strip* at the gathering tape on the lining side of the panel.

(d.) Secure it to the P.L. Strip* with thumbtacks to the front (drapery side).

(e.) Then hot glue or fabric glue the velcro to the P.L. Strip* on the back (lining side).

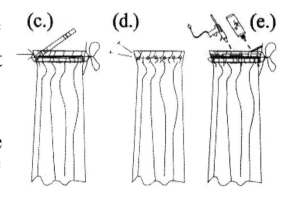

Rod Pocket Sleeve Panel

The rod pocket sleeve method is used with the 3 piece connected P.L. Strip* (see (b.) on page 125). To make the rod pocket sleeve,

(a.) turn the top of the panel over 1 " to the lining side, press then turn over the top another 2" press again.
(b.) Straight stich or Heat and bond a rod pocket sleeve to fit over the 3 pieces of connected P.L. Strips*.

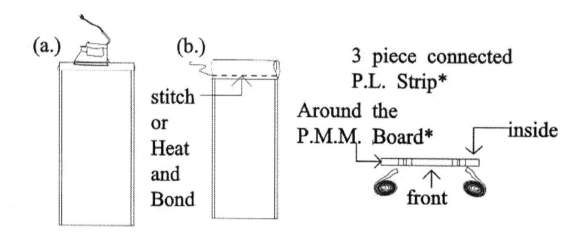

(b.) Gather the rod pocket sleeve over the connected P.L. Strips*.

(c.) Arrange the gathers evenly then thumbtack the gathers in place on the lining side of the panel. Hot glue or use fabric glue to secure the velcro over the thumbtacks.

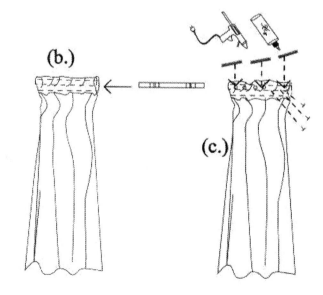

Box Pleat Panel

The box pleat is directly applied to the 3 pieces of P.L. Strip* connected with masking tape (see (b.) page 125). To finish the raw ends of the top of the drapery panel, turn the top over 1 1/2" twice, press, then straight stitch a 1 1 /2" hem (see (a.) page 124).

(a.) Take the 3 pieces of the P.L. Strip* connected with masking tape and lay them out flat.

(b.) Take the top of the drapery panel, with the wrong side down on the connected P.L. Strip*, and start at each of the outside edges, make two box pleats. Hold the pleats in place on the P.L. Strip* with the thumbtacks placed on the front (drapery side). When finished with the two outside edges,

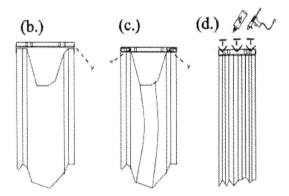

(c.) then start at the very middle of the panel and box pleat the middle, then take each half, made by the box pleat in the middle, and continue to box pleat each half until the entire panel has been pleated.

(d.) Hot glue or apply fabric glue to secure the velcro to the P.L. Strip* on the back (lining side).

(a.) Regardless of which method was used to gather the drapery panels and apply the velcro, the application to the short side boards will be the same. Marry the velcro of the drapery panels to the short side board, front to front, inside to inside, and the outside to the outside of the P.M.M. Board*.

(b.) After the panels have been applied to the short side boards, measure and pin up a double 6" bottom hem. The drapery panels can then be removed to be hemmed either by hand, by using the blind hem stitch selector on the sewing machine, or by using iron on hem binding tape. If preferred, they too can be puddled on the floor.

(c.) Use lead weighted tape in the bottom of the hem to make the drapery panel hang better. After hemming, then attach a large safety pin to one end of the weighted tape.

(d.) Slip it through one end of the hem to the other end.

(e.) Cut the end to the width of the panel.

(f.) Whipstitch the ends in place to the wrong side of the panel.

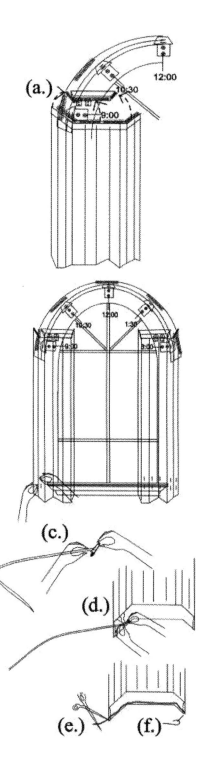

(a.) To encourage distinct folds in the drapery panel, fan fold the panel with a "sideways U" bent finger formation to make folds go in and out. Wrap scrap pieces of fabric around the folds, to hold them in place. Place them at the top, middle, and bottom of the drapery panel. Allow to stand for 2 to 3 days.

(b.) After removing the scrap pieces of fabric utilized to hold the folds, use a steam iron to remove wrinkles and make the folds smooth. Stand back and evaluate for symmetry and fullness, fluff and puff as needed.

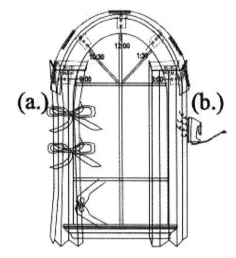

Apply the top treatment after the two short side boards have been mounted. Arrange the Swaged Lattice so that the drapery panels will be under the swags but over the P.L. Strip* of the Swaged Lattice. Apply extra velcro any places that are needed so curtains lay smooth.

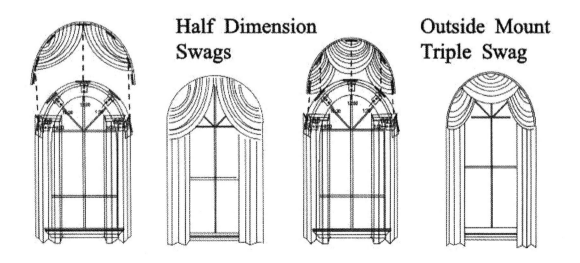

Half Dimension Swags

Outside Mount Triple Swag

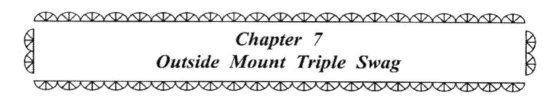

Chapter 7
Outside Mount Triple Swag

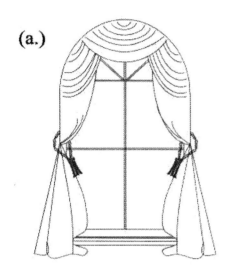

(a.)

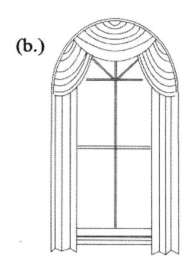

(b.)

This chapter addresses the top treatment "Outside Mount Triple Swag" and the various ways it can be applied. The two different applications are shown in figure

(a.) "Outside Mount Triple Swag With Rod Pocket Sleeve" and figure

(b.) "Outside Mount Triple Swag With Two Short Side Boards. Look over each of the applications to choose the one which will be best suited for your window's needs.

The following chapter "Half Dimensions Swags", will show how to make your own swags, using your own pattern.

* Polystyrene Lattice Strip abbreviated as P.L. Strip*
* Polystyrene Moulding Mounting Board abbreviated as P.M.M. Board*

Check List For Tools and Supplies

* Drapery fabric
* Lining fabric
* Matching thread
* For No Sew = 1 roll of each 3/4" and 1/4" Heat and Bond
* Short thumbtacks
* Masking tape
* Hot glue gun
* Fabric glue
* Velcro
* P.L. Strip*
* Swag Pattern
* Or follow Swag Pattern in chapter 8 "Half Dimension Swags"
* Directions for chapter 5 "Rod Pocket Sleeve Drapery Panels with a Diagonal Cut to Fit Arched Windows" or
* Directions for chapter 6 "Two Short Side Boards Drapery Panels"
* Iron
* Sissors
* Tape measure
* Dissappearing ink pen

Depending on the window size, most swag patterns can be adapted, or even store bought ready made swags and drapery panels can be customized. The following pages give drapery yardage estimations and instructions for customizing ready made store bought drapes.

Drapery and Lining Yardage Estimation

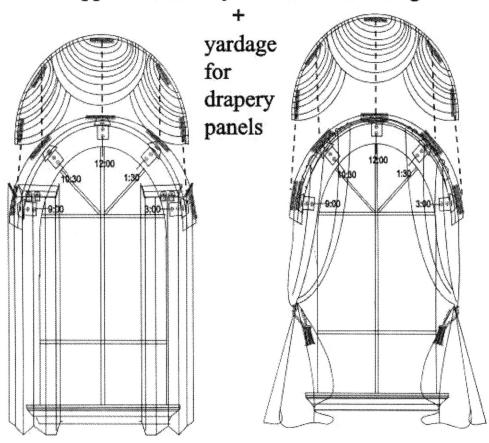

Approximate 2 yards for each swag
+
yardage for drapery panels

Approximate 2 yards for each swag for each the drapery and lining fabric. If using a swag pattern then check the instructions for fabric yardage for that particular pattern. Plus add the yardage for the drapery panels. For drapery panel yardage see chapter 5, "Rod Pocket Sleeve with Diagonal Cut for Arched Windows" or chapter 6, "Two Short Side Boards Drapery Panels". It is recommended to make a test swag out of muslin or an old bed sheet to check for appropriate swag width and drop size for the window size.

Customising Store Bought Drapes

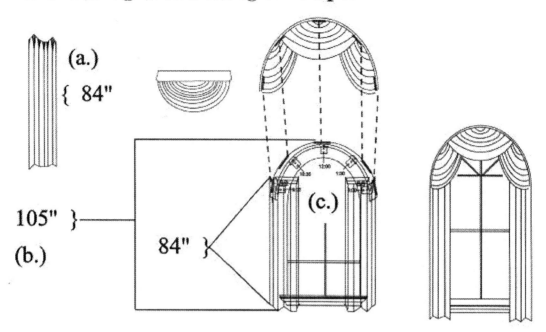

(a.) If you are using store bought ready made curtains (swags and drapery panels), more than likely your drapery panels will be only 84" long, because 84" is the longest length for standard curtains. Many of the half round windows that are so popular with new home designs today have windows much taller than the standard 84 ".

(b.) Even with arched windows as tall as 105", you can adapt the store bought ready made curtain for a custom made look. Just be sure the swags are large enough to come down to cover the short side board panels.

(c.) Using the "Two Short Side Boards Drapery Panels" will be the easiest application for this treatment. This will be a stationary window treatment for show only, not a functional curtain, but considering the time saved in not sewing and the minimal amount of alterations to be done, will make it one of the easiest arched window treatments of them all!

Customising Store Bought Drapes

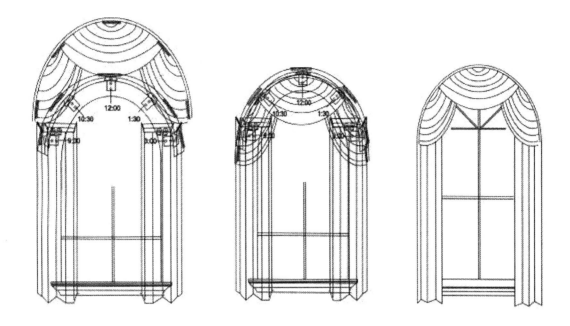

For store bought ready made swags follow the general outline on the following pages for the swag application to the P.L. Strip*. There will two choices in how to mount the "Outside Mount Triple Swag" top treatment, the "Swag Lattice Turned Over" and the Swag Lattice with Cover", see page 136. If using the "Swag Lattice with Cover" then purchase and extra drapery panel to make the cover and see chapter 4 the section "Covered Jute Webbing" (pages 67 to 78) or "Simply Covered Crinoline" (pages 79 to 84).

For the drapery panel application of the store bought ready made drapes, follow the general outline in the chapter 6, "Two Short Board Side Boards Drapery Panels".

Overall View

There are two finishes to the top treatment "Outside Mount Triple Swag", (a.) the "Swag Lattice Turned Over" and (b.) the "Swag Lattice with Cover". Read through each of the finishes in the following pages, before starting to determine which one is preferred, each will vary slightly in the application. Below shows a quick overview of each.

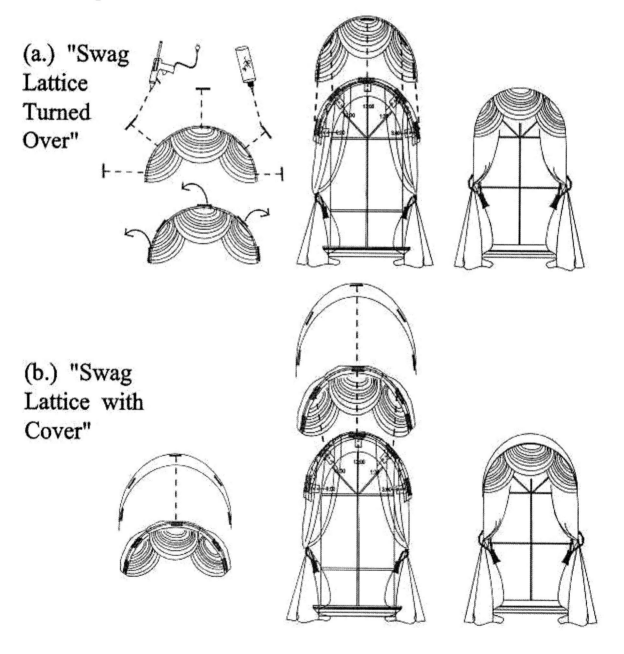

(a.) "Swag Lattice Turned Over"

(b.) "Swag Lattice with Cover"

The "Outside Mount Triple Swag" is made of 3 identically made swags and mounted onto a P.L. Strip* held in place by thumbtacks.

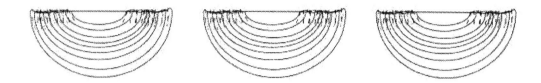

If the swags are large and deep enough then they can be directly applied to the P.L. Strip* and held in place with thumbtacks. If you are following the swag pattern in, chapter 8 "Half Dimension Swags" a tab may not be necessary, depending on the size of the swag. The basic square should be smaller than the 54" x 54", which makes a very large swag. When using 3 swags, a smaller size will be needed especially if you have a smaller window. Make a test swag and make adjustments as needed.

1 = Thumbtack
2 = Velcro
3 = P.L. Strip*

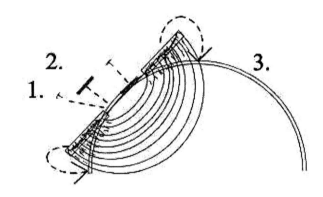

However with most of the swag patterns the addition of a tab to the top of the swag will be needed to allow for more working room with the middle of the swag when it is applied to the P.L. Strip*. The addition of the tab will most likely be needed for the finish "Swag Lattice with Cover", the following pages give details for making a tab.

To make the tab to the top of the swag first make the swags, follow your swag pattern to make 3 matching swags. Designer tip: to add more body to the swag, use Craft Bond Pellon or similar type product, ironed and bonded only to the lining side of the swag. Place the side of the lining with the ironed on Craft Bonded Pellon so it will be inside of the swag, facing the wrong side of the drapery fabric. This trick works best with a swag pattern where the fabric is "cut on the bias". However it is not recommended for the top treatment "Swag Lattice Turned Over".

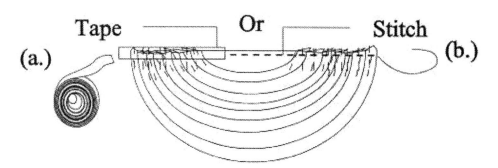

When folds of the swag are pulled up and complete then secure the folds at the top.

(a.) If you are using the no sew method adjust and pin folds evenly, and once the folds are adjusted and even then secure them with masking tape at the very top of the swag, then turn swag over and secure the back side of the folds with tape at the top. Leave pins in place until swag is secured to the P.L Strip* with thumbtacks, then the pins and tape can be removed.

(b.) If you are using the sewing method then secure folds at the top with pins. Make sure all the swags are the same, and then stitch straight tiny a 1 /4" seam allowance across the very top of the folds, then remove the pins.

(a.) After the top of the swag has been secured with tape or stitching then cut the tab to fit the swag. Cut a 3 1/2" strip of drapery material 1" longer than the top edge of the swag. This is to accommodate a 1/2" side hem for each side and 1 /2" hem for one long side. If the fabric unravels easily, an over lock stitch may be needed.

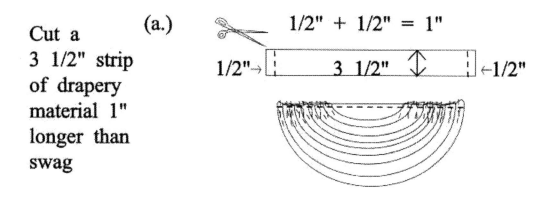

Cut a 3 1/2" strip of drapery material 1" longer than swag

(b.) Turn under and stitch or Heat and Bond a 1/2" hem on 3 sides (the 2 short sides and 1 long side). The other long side will be attached to the top of the swag.

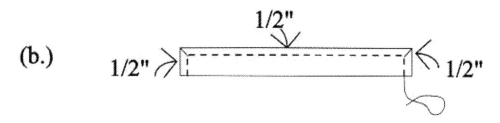

Stitch or Heat and Bond 1/2" hem on 3 sides

(a.) When finished hemming the 3 sides then place the unhemmed long side, even with the top edge of the swag and place right sides together and pin.

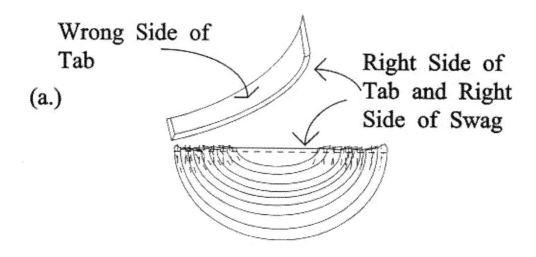

(b.) Stitch a tiny 1/4" seam allowance along the top edge of the swag.

(c.) If the no sew method was used then bond the tab to the top of the swag using 1/4" Heat and Bond. Carefully remove the tape on the front of the swag, and move the pins farther down out of the way of the Heat and Bond as you go.

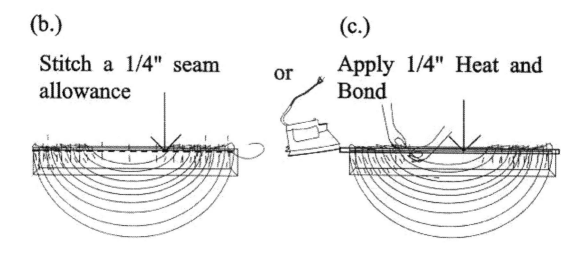

(a.) If the drapery material unravels easily, a three stitch zig zag or overlock stitch may be needed along the edge of the swag and the tab. An overlock stitch is often difficult to undo, so be sure the swags and tab appear satisfactory before stitching in an overlock stitch. "Fray Stop" (or similar product) applied to the edge may be another alternative to an overlock stitch.

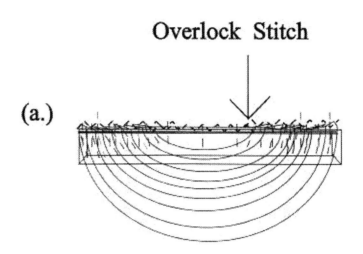

(b.) If the no sew method was used, the adhesion of the Heat and Bond may be enough to keep the edge from unraveling. If not then apply Fray or similar product to the edges.

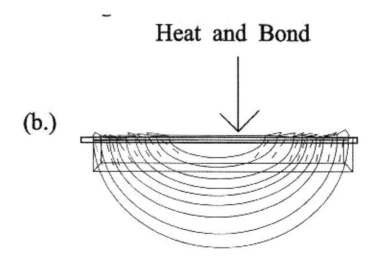

(a.) Iron the seam of the top of the swag and tab flat Use a pressing cloth or pillow case to keep from possibly scorching the drapery fabric.

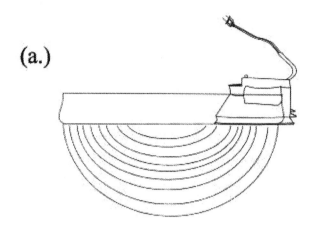

(b.) The top outer side edges of the swag will greatly over lap the P.L. Strip*. The tab is needed to lengthen the drapery material at the middle of the swag, so as the P.L. Strip* is turned over to be placed down onto the P.M.M. Board*, that as much of the swag as possible will be showing.

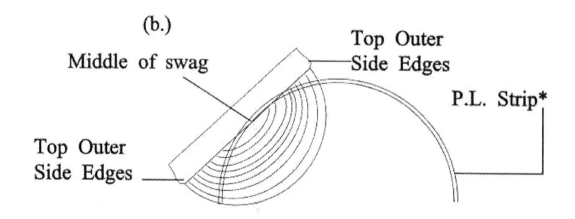

(a.) Be sure and try and make your swags as identical to each other as possible. Inspect the swags, note symmetry and slight defects etc. Measure the swags to see how close in size they are, position the two that are the most exact in size on each of the outer edges.

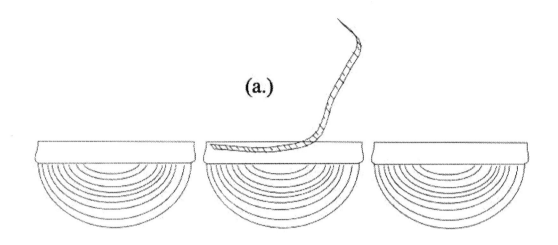

(b.) If all the swags are the exactly the same in size then position the one that is the most symmetrical in the center. After deciding which swag will be center and which one will be right and left swag, then mark C. R. and L. (for center, right, and left) with an invisible pen or mark very lightly with a pencil, on the back of the swag in a hidden area.

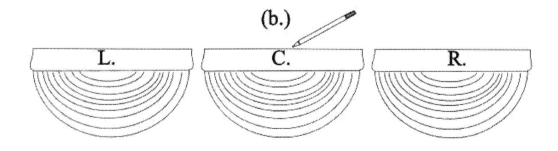

(a.) Using a pencil or pen mark the exact center of the P.L. Strip* by measuring the entire length of the P.L. Strip* to the nearest 1/8", then divide this number by 2. A calculator may be helpful when dividing fractions of an inch (1 /8" = 0.125, 1 /4" = 0.25, 1 /2" = 0.50), or if there is metric side to the tape measure use it for easy calculations.

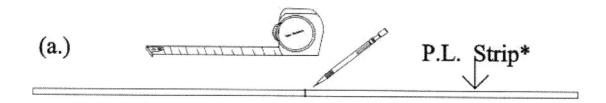

It is important to find and mark the exact middle of the P.L. Strip*. This is because it will be the point of reference especially for the middle swag, so the Triple Swag application will appear symmetrical and balanced.

Before applying the swags to the P.L. Strip* first decide if you prefer the finish "Swag Lattice Turned Over" or "Swag Lattice with Cover". If you have chosen the "Swag Lattice Turned Over", then continue on. If you have chosen the "Swag Lattice with Cover", then look ahead to page 161 to see how they are applied by fully utilizing the tab extension you have applied to the swags. Other than fully utilizing the tab extension the "Swag Lattice with Cover" will basically be applied to the P.L. Strip* in the same manner as the "Swag Lattice Turned Over".

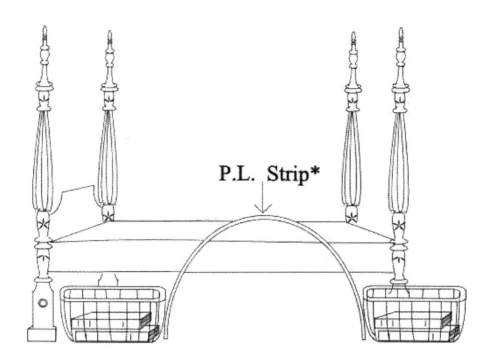

A good place to work with your P.L. Strip* and swag is next to a bed or table where you can lean the P.L. Strip* so it will stand upright in a curved form position. Use 2 objects to keep the ends of the P.L. Strip* from slipping away. One example could be 2 laundry baskets with clothes or books in them for weight. Approximate the width of the window and place the laundry baskets that far apart next to the bed or table. Bend the P.L. Strip* so each end rests on the carpet against the laundry baskets. Let the P.L. Strip* lean against the bed or table. This will keep it in a upright position. You will need to work with the P.L. Strip* bent in the upright position because in this position you can approximate the curve of your window. If you try and work with the P.L. Strip* flat all the time it will be harder to see how the curtain is likely to hang.

(a.) You can, if you like, approximate the swags on the P.L. Strip* in how you think will be attractive for your window treatment, keep them held lightly in place on the P.L. Strip* with thumbtacks. Note, measure, and lightly mark where the bottom edge of the right and left swag are from the ends of the P.L. Strip*.

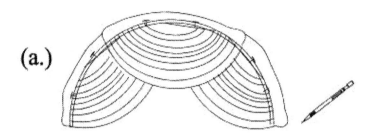

(b.) A good rule of thumb is for the bottom edge of the outer swags to be positioned 3 to 8 inches past the 3:00 and 9:00 o'clock positions. The 3:00 and 9:00 o'clock positions also coordinate with the straight horizontal top aluminum casing for the square glass window pane that are on many of the half round windows.

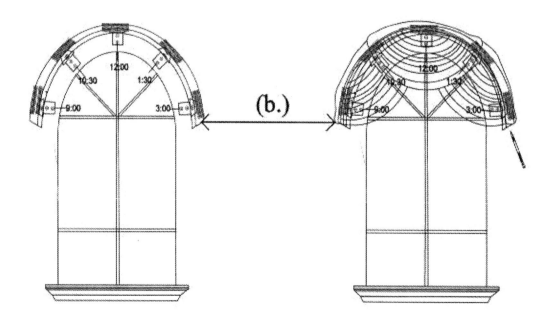

(a.) Remove the swags and measure exactly how far from each end of the P.L. Strip* the swags hang, then remark the right and left sides on the P.L. Strip* to be the exact same measurement. This will indicate where the bottom edge of the outer swag will stop. This will help ensure the curtain swags will be evenly balanced.

(a.)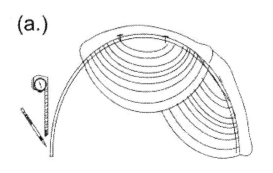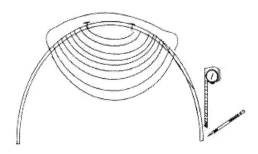

(b.) Double check and be sure the measurement from the end of the P.L. Strip* to the end of the where the bottom edge of the outer swags stop is the same on both sides.

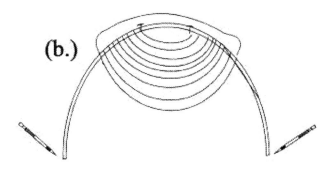

If you do not want to bother with the trial run of "just seeing how the swags are going to look", then:

(a.) Hold the P.L. Strip* up to the P.M.M. Board*, line up the center of the P.M.M. Board* to the center of the P.L. Strip*.

(b.) Have a partner mark where the 3:00 and the 9:00 o'clock positions are.

(c.) After a rough estimate where the 3:00 and the 9:00 o'clock positions are, then go back and remark the 9:00 o'clock position to be the exact same measurement from the end as the 3:00 o'clock position or vice versa. This will help ensure the curtain swags will be evenly balanced.

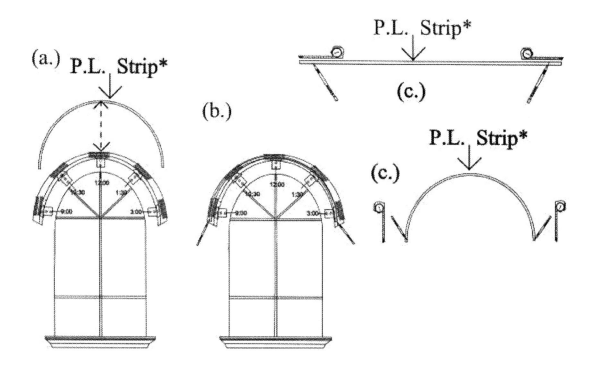

The shape of the swag is round on the bottom but the shape at the top is straight across. This straight edge will need to be rounded off so it will fit on a round window.

(a.) To round off the outer edges of the swag arrange it on the P.L. Strip* so that the right and left top outer ends of each swag will hang over the P.L. Strip* by 2" to 3".

(b.) The middle of the swag will barley cover the edge of the P.L. Strip*, so when it is in the half round curved form, the swag will conform to this shape.

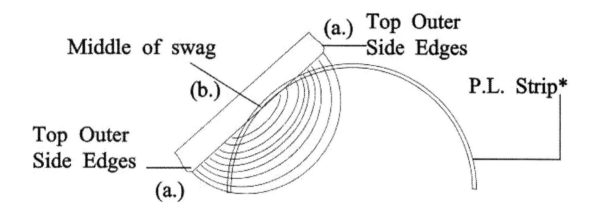

Again a good place to work with your P.L. Strip* is next to a bed or table where you can lean the P.L. Strip* so it will stand upright in a curved form position. With the P.L. Strip* in the upright bent position apply the outer swags first.

Use the marks made from measuring up from the end of the P.L. Strip* as guidelines where the outer edges of the swags will be positioned.

(a.) Starting with the left outer swag, place the top left end of the swag 2" to 3" over the edge of the P.L. Strip* but line up the curved bottom edge of the swag even with the mark you made when you measured up from the ends.

(b.) The other top end of the swag will also lie 2" to 3" over the edge of the P.L. Strip* and the middle of the swag will barely cover over the edge of the P.L. Strip*.

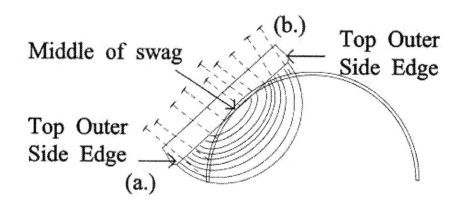

(c.) Thumbtack = T

(c.) Secure the swag to the P.L. Strip* with short thumbtacks, be sure to use short thumbtacks. Place a thumbtack at least every other fold, or at every fold if necessary, and place 2 to 3 thumbtacks in the middle of the swag. Make sure the folds lay flat and the swag hangs nicely, readjust as needed.

(a.) Repeat exactly the same, but in reverse, to the right side of the P.L. Strip* with the right swag.

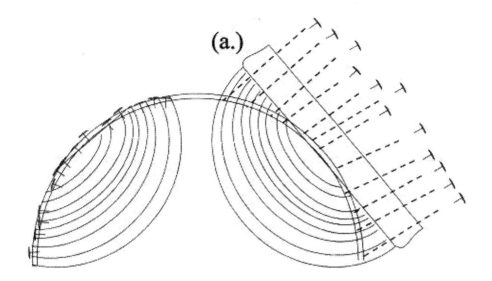

(b.) When finished, the top edge of the right and left swags should be equal distance from the center mark on the P.L. Strip*. If not then pull taught or slacken the swags untill each are an exact distance from the center mark of the P.L. Strip*.

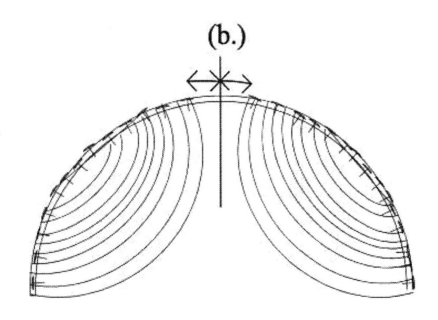

(a.) To apply the center swag, use a cloth tape measure and measure the top inside fold of the center swag itself, divide this number by 2 to find the middle of the center fold.

(b.) Mark this spot with a disappearing ink pen.

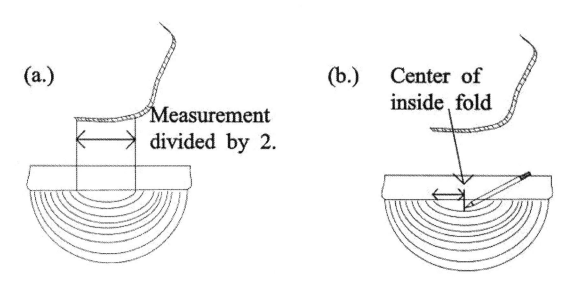

(c.) Now fold the entire swag in half to find the center of the entire swag. Mark each with a different notation, so you can distinguish which is the middle of the center fold and which is the center of the entire swag. The mark made on the swag that indicates the center of the entire swag is a reference point in deciding which way the swag should "lean" to keep it looking perfectly centered on the P.L. Strip*.

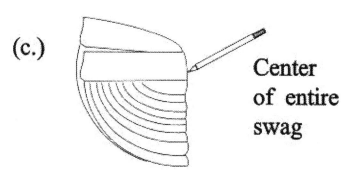

Be sure the mark made for the exact center of the P.L. Strip* is well defined.

(a.) Place a thumbtack in the tab, near the top edge of the swag on the mark made for the middle of the center fold of the swag.

(b.) Place the thumbtack and swag in the center mark made on the P.L. Strip*, this should line up the center of the swag with the center of the P.L. Strip*. The mark made on the swag that indicates the center of the entire swag is a reference point in deciding which way the swag should "lean" to keep it looking perfectly centered on the P.L. Strip*.

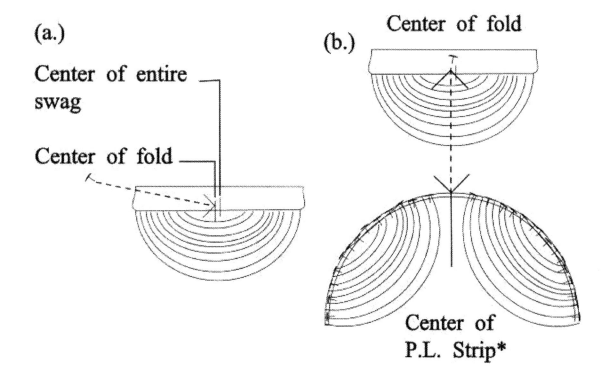

As with the outer swags, the center swag will

(a.) also need to have the top outer ends rounded off by having them hang 2" to 3" off the P.L. Strip* with the middle of the swag barely covering the P.L. Strip*. The center swag should be positioned evenly over the right and left swag.

(b.) Count which fold of the right and left swag, the edge of the center swag lies on top of. For example if the left edge of the center swag lies on top of the fourth fold on the left sided swag then the right edge of the center swag should lie on top of the fourth fold of the right sided swag. If this doesn't happen then readjust, by a slight tightening or slackening of the center swag. If there is still too much of a difference then recheck the size of the right and left swags. If there is more than 1 /2" difference in the sizes then you may need to repin the folds of the swags to approximate a more exact closeness in size. If you are working with store bought ready made swags, then they are likely to be equal in size and this should not be a problem.

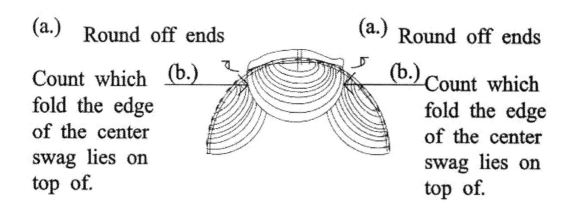

As mentioned the finish of the "Outside Mount Triple Swag" can done in one of two ways.

(a.) One is the "Swaged Lattice Turned Over" where the side of the P.L. Strip* with the thumbtacks will be turned over one time. In this application the swags should be long enough to have enough room to be folded over the P.L. Strip*, plus another 3 1/4" to inches to clear the P.M.M. Board*.

(b.) The second is the "Swaged Lattice With Cover" where the side of the P.L. Strip* with the thumbtacks, will be left face up, not turned over. The P.L. Strip* and tabs of the swags will be covered with a Covered Jute Webbing, or a Simply Covered Crinoline.

Each of these will be discussed in the following pages. Read through each one to decide which finish best suits your window's dressing needs.

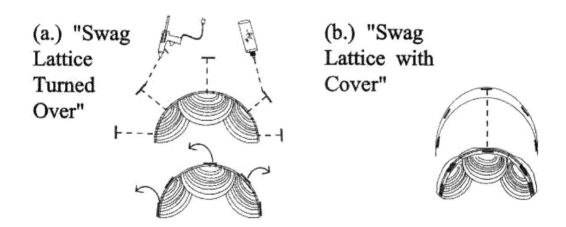

(a.) "Swag Lattice Turned Over"

(b.) "Swag Lattice with Cover"

The former finish "Swaged Lattice Turned Over", shall be addressed first. Put the swaged P.L. Strip* through a test run to see how the swags hang, etc.

(a.) When satisfied, then apply the velcro to the 12:00, 1:30, 10:30, 3:00, and 9:00, o'clock positions. Use hot glue or fabric glue and thumbtacks to hold the velcro strips in place.

(b.) Turn the swaged P.L. Strip* over one time so .the velcro and the thumbtacks will be face down.

(c.) The velcro and the thumbtacks should all be hidden underneath, and only the graceful folds of the swag are visible.

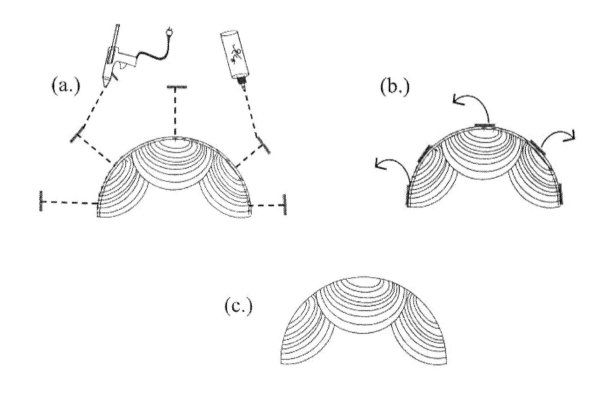

The velcro of the "Swaged Lattice Turned Over" will marry to the velcro at the coordinating positions on the back edge of the P.M.M. Board* (next to the wall). But first apply either (a.) or (b.).

(a.) "Two Short Side Boards" drapery panels, which are applied to the side, see chapter 6.

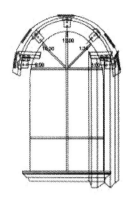 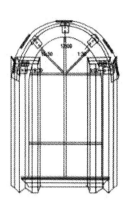

(b.) Or the "Rod Pocket Sleeve Drapery Panels with a Diagonal Cut to Fit Arched Windows", which are applied to the velcro at the front of the P.M.M. Board*, see chapter 5.

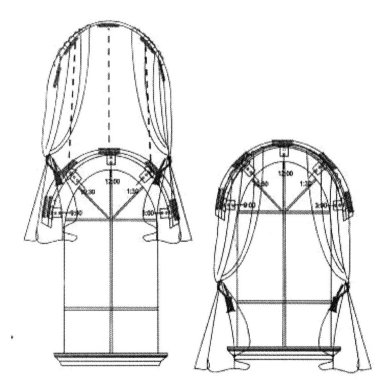

As mentioned, apply the drapery panels first. After the "Swag Lattice Turned Over" has been turned over one time, readjust the folds of the swag so they lay smooth and neat.

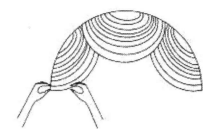

Then marry the velcro of the "Swaged Lattice Turned Over" down to the velcro at the coordinating positions on the back edge of the P.M.M. Board* (next to the wall).

(a.) The "Two Short Side Boards Drapery Panels" or

(b.) The "Rod Pocket Sleeve Drapery Panels with a Diagonal Cut to Fit Arched Windows".

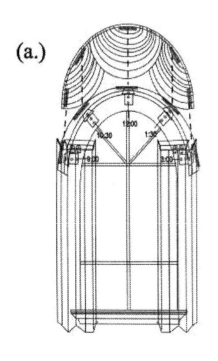
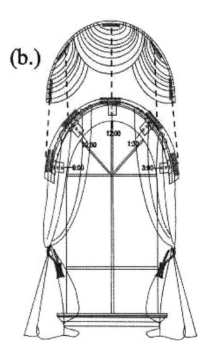

Since the under drapery panels are in front of the swags, there will be a small space left showing the swaged P.L. Strip* and the P.M.M. Board*.

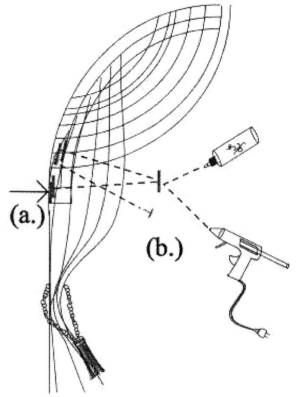

(a.) To correct this apply small strips of velcro or thumbtacks to marry both the edge of the drapery panel to the P.L. Strip* of the top treatment.

(b.) Place the velcro on the wrong side of the drapery panel along the side hem line. Start placing the marrying velcro up under the top treatment and continue as needed untill the panel flows down the side of the P.M.M. Board* evenly. Spot weld marrying velcro or thumbtack any spots as needed.

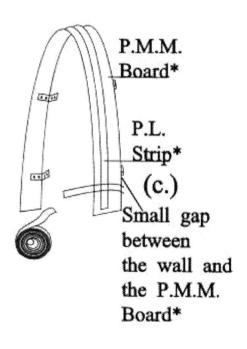

(c.) To secure the very end of the P.L. Strip* to the end of the P.M.M. Board*, slip a strip of 1" masking tape up in the small gap between the wall and the P.M.M. Board*. Wrap the tape completely around the two ends. Here it is shown illustrated without the drapery treatment, but do this after the drapery treatment has been applied.

Apply tie backs for a polished look to the "Rod Pocket Sleeve Drapery Panels". Sheers and or miniblinds can be placed underneath the curtains for privacy and light control.

"Swag Lattice Turned Over"

The following pages will address the second finish of the "Outside Mount Triple Swag", named the "Swag Lattice With Cover".

"Swag Lattice with Cover"

The other finish to the swaged lattice is the "Swag Lattice With Cover". In this application the swaged P.L. Strip* is left face up and a cover is added to hide the thumbtacks etc. To make either of the covers follow the instructions as directed in chapter 4 "No Sew Gathered Sheet Drapes with a Covered Jute Webbing" and see the section regarding the "Covered Jute Webbing" pages 67 to 78, or the "Simply Covered Crinoline" pages 79 to 84.

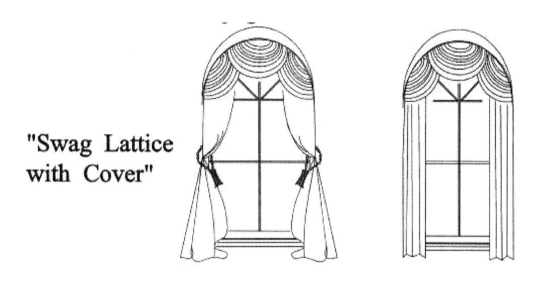

When applying the swags and tab extensions for the "Swag Lattice With Cover" you will be utilizing most of the tab extension so most of the swag will fall to the front and over the P.M.M. Board*.

Follow the same basic procedure as detailed earlier in this chapter for the "Swag Lattice Turned Over" regarding the application of the swags to the P.L. Strip* only use most of the tab extension of the swag. The following pages will detail the "Swag Lattice With Cover".

To apply the swags and tab extensions for the "Swag Lattice With Cover"

(a.) Still round off the top outer edges by allowing the outer ends of each swag to hang over the P.L. Strip* by only 1 /2" to 1 1 /2", but the middlle of the swag will have most of the tab extention showing.

(b.) Find the center of the swag and mark the center across the tab with dissappearing ink pen.

(c.) Place a thumbtack in the middle of the tab near the back of the tab and place the thumbtack and swag on the mark made for the middle of the P.L. Strip*.

(d.) Apply thumbtacks to hold the swags in place as detailed earlier.

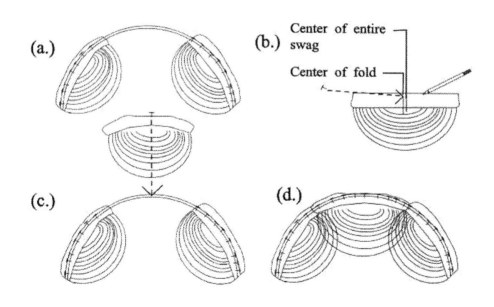

With the "Swag Lattice With Cover" you will be applying velcro to both the top and the underside of the swaged P.L. Strip*. Use hot glue or fabric glue and thumbtacks to apply the velcro.

(a.) On the top of the "Swag Lattice With Cover" apply 4" to 6" strips of velcro to the 12:00, 1:30, 10:30, 3:00, and 9:00 o'clock positions and at the very ends, that will marry to the velcro that is placed on the underside of the cover.

(b.) On the underside of the "Swag Lattice With Cover" apply 4" to 6" strips of velcro to the 12:00, 1:30, 10:30, 3:00, and 9:00 o'clock positions and at the very ends, that will marry to the velcro on top of the P.M.M. Board*.

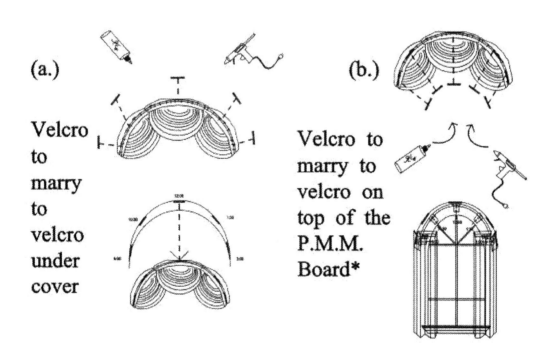

(a.) Velcro to marry to velcro under cover

(b.) Velcro to marry to velcro on top of the P.M.M. Board*

(a.) Find the exact center of the "Covered Jute Webbing" or the "Simply Covered Crinoline" by measuring the entire length of the cover to the nearest 1/8", then divide this number by 2. A calculator may be helpful when dividing fractions of an inch (1/8" _ 0.125, 1/4" = 0.25, 1/2" = 0.50). Or for easy calculations use the metric side of the tape measure. On the underside of the cover lightly mark the center spot with, a pencil, or preferably a disappearing ink pen, and apply a 4" to 6" strip of velcro on the underside, to the back of the center mark of the cover.

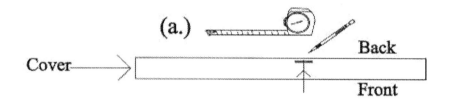

(b.) Place 4" to 6" strips of velcro to the rest of the coordinating o'clock positions (1:30, 10:30, 3:00, and 9:00 o'clock) and at the very ends on the underside at the back of the cover ("Covered Jute Webbing" or the "Simply Covered Crinoline") so it will marry to the velcro on top of the "Swag Lattice With Cover". Apply extra married up velcro as needed to the Drapery Panel P.L. Strip* or any other areas so the cover will lay smooth. When satisfied go back and glue in place.

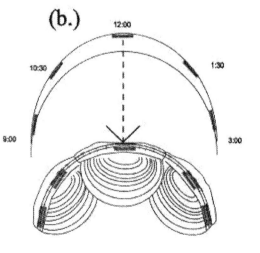

The velcro under the "Rod Pocket Sleeve Drapery Panel"

(a.) will marry to the front edge of the P.M.M. Board*. The velcro under the swaged P.L. Strip*

(b.) will marry to the velcro on the back edge of the P.M.M. Board*. The velcro under the Covered Jute Webbing or Simply Covered Crinoline

(c.) will marry to the velcro on top of the swaged P.L. Strip*. Add extra married up velcro and or thumbtacks as needed to the top of the Drapery Panel P.L. Strip* and any other areas needed, so the cover lays smooth and flat.

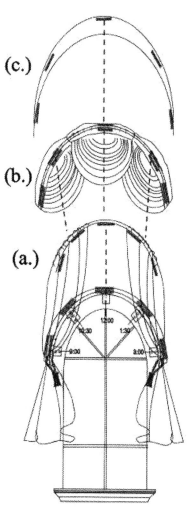

(c.) Covered Jute Webbing or Simply Covered Crinoline

(b.) Swaged P.L. Strip*

(a.) "Rod Pocket Sleeve Drapery Panels with Diagonal Cut to Fit Arched Windows" P.L. Strip* (a.) To correct this apply small strips of velcro or thumbtacks to marry both the edge of the drapery panel to the P.L. Strip* of the top treatment.

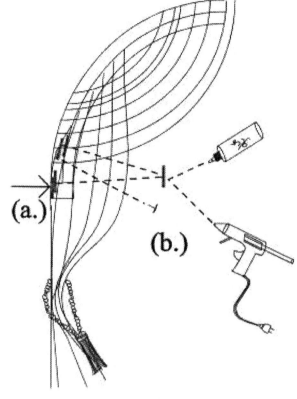

(b.) Place the velcro on the wrong side of the drapery panel along the side hem line. Start placing the marrying velcro up under the top treatment and continue as needed until the panel flows down the side of the P.M.M. Board* evenly. Spot weld marrying velcro or thumbtack any spots as needed.

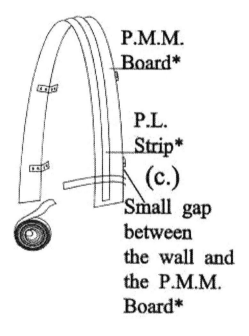

(c.) To secure the very end of the P.L. Strip* to the end of the P.M.M. Board*, slip a strip of 1" masking tape up in the small gap between the wall and the P.M.M. Board*. Wrap the tape completely around the two ends. Here it is shown illustrated without the drapery treatment, but do this after the drapery treatment has been applied.

Similarly for the "Two Short Side Boards Drapery Panels", the velcro under the swaged P.L. Strip*,

(a.) will marrry to the velcro at the back edge of the P.M.M. Board*. The velcro under the Covered Jute Webbing or Simply Covered Crinoline

(b.) will marry to the velcro on top of the swaged P.L. Strip*.

Add extra velcro and or thumbtacks to any areas needed to secure the cover to the P.L. Strip*, so it will lay smooth and flat.

(b.) Covered Jute Webbing or Simply Covered Crinoline

(a.) Swaged P.L. Strip*

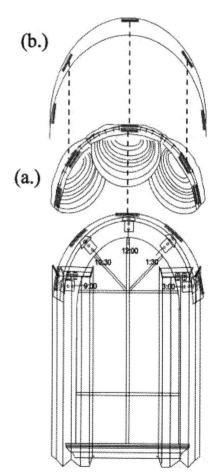

"Swag Lattice with Cover"

Stand back and evaluate for symmetry and smoothness of the folds and swags. Tuck, fold, pin, whipstitch, velcro, thumbtack, fluff and, or puff as needed.

For privacy apply sheers and or miniblinds.

Chapter 8
Half Dimension Swags

In this chapter we will show how to make your own swag pattern using a square of fabric and masking tape as a cutting guide. Half Dimension Swags is given its name by how the swag is achieved. Each swag covers half of an arch, as well as being achieved by dividing various half dimensions of a square. Frequently drapery fabric widths are 54". This swag is based on that width. This makes a very large swag. Often it is hard to find drapery patterns to make a swag this large. Smaller swags can be made by using a smaller square.

* Polystyrene Lattice Strip abbreviated as P.L. Strip*
* Polystyrene Moulding Mounting Board abbreviated as
  P.M.M. Board*

Checklist for Tools and Supplies

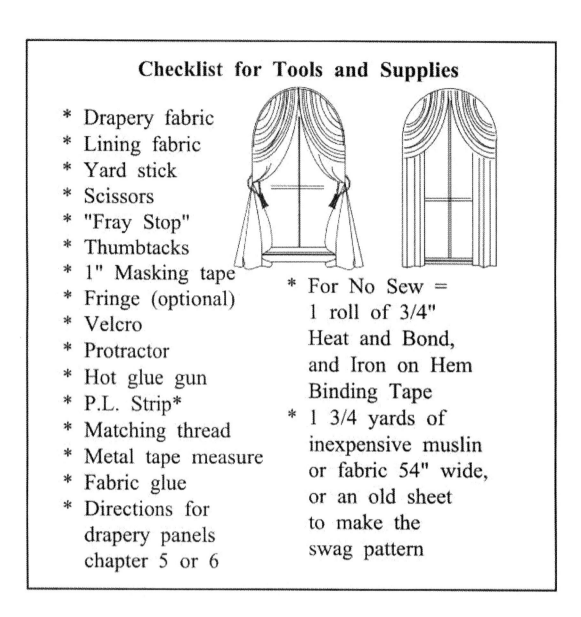

* Drapery fabric
* Lining fabric
* Yard stick
* Scissors
* "Fray Stop"
* Thumbtacks
* 1" Masking tape
* Fringe (optional)
* Velcro
* Protractor
* Hot glue gun
* P.L. Strip*
* Matching thread
* Metal tape measure
* Fabric glue
* Directions for drapery panels chapter 5 or 6
* For No Sew = 1 roll of 3/4" Heat and Bond, and Iron on Hem Binding Tape
* 1 3/4 yards of inexpensive muslin or fabric 54" wide, or an old sheet to make the swag pattern

The instructions in this chapter mainly pertain to the top treatment of the "Half Dimension Swags". For the under treatment drapery panel application turn to chapter 5 "Rod Pocket Sleeve Drapery Panels with Diagonal Cut To Fit Arched Windows" or chapter 6" Two Short Side Boards Drapery Panels". See the following page for drapery yardage estimations.

Drapery and Lining Fabric Yardage Estimation

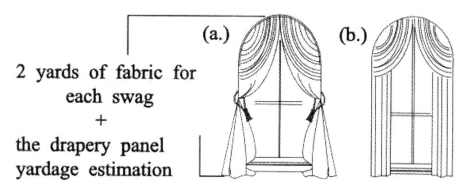

2 yards of fabric for each swag
+
the drapery panel yardage estimation

For this window treatment a very large swag is needed, especially for the larger windows. The largest square possible for a 54" width fabric is 54" x 54" (estimate 2 yards of fabric for each swag, for each the drapery and lining fabric. For one window treatment 2 swags = 4 yards of each fabric allowing a little extra room to straighten the edge of the fabric etc. Then add the amount needed for the chosen under drapery panel treatment. It is always better to have a little too much fabric than come up a little too short.

For the drapery panel yardage estimation turn to the

(a.) chapter 5 "Rod Pocket Sleeve Drapery Panels with Diagonal Cut To Fit Arched Windows" or

(b.) chapter 6 "Two Short Side Boards Drapery Panels".

It will be necessary to first make a test swag out of 54" wide inexpensive muslin, fabric, or an old bed sheet. This test swag will then become the pattern swag for the rest of the swags.

To use this same make your own swag pattern for other window treatments such as the "Single Swag and the "Outside Mount Triple Swag", then use a smaller square size 48" x 48", depending on your window size.

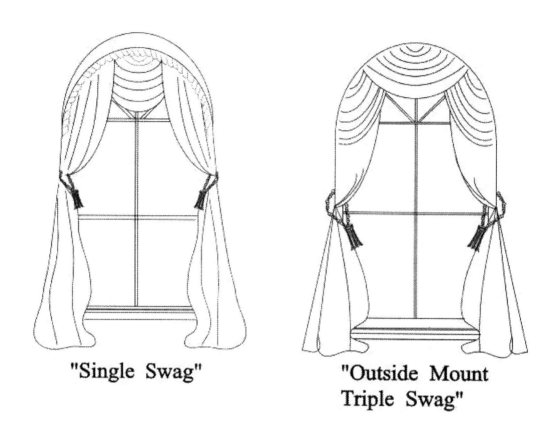

"Single Swag"   "Outside Mount Triple Swag"

As mentioned, it will be necessary to first make a test swag out of inexpensive muslin or an old bed sheet. Once satisfied with the test swag, it then becomes the pattern swag for which to make all the rest of the swags. The following pages show how to form the test swag from a square of fabric (54" muslin, inexpensive fabric, or an old bed sheet).

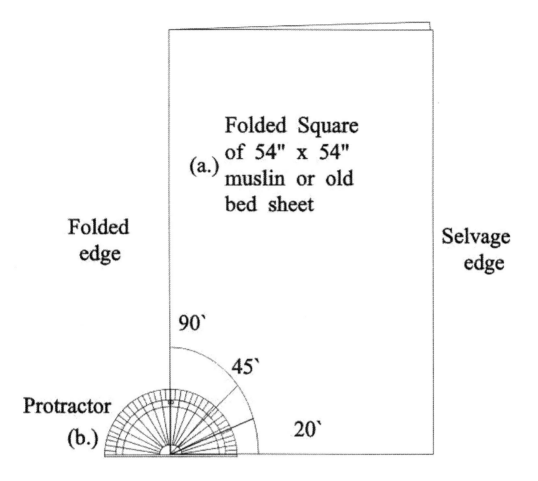

(a.) Using the inexpensive 54" muslin or an old sheet, cut a true square 54" x 54". Fold the square in half, selvage edge to selvage edge. Place the folded edge on the left and the selvage edge on the right.

(b.) The square folded in half still has right angles at each corner and each right angle equals 90 degrees. Half of 90 degrees is 45 degrees and half of 45 degrees is 22 1/2 degrees. Approximately 20 to 22 1/2 degrees will be the mark in which to place the first strip of masking tape. It may be helpful to use a protractor.

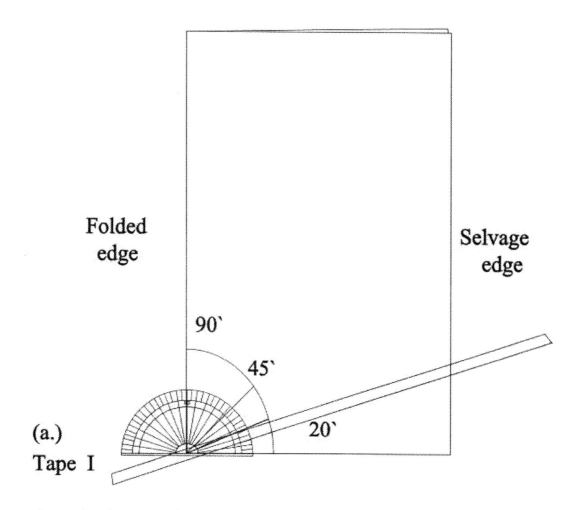

One inch masking tape is used to mark and make the guidelines in which to cut the material. (a.) Using the bottom left corner of the folded square, which is on the folded side, place a strip of 1" masking tape starting at the very tip of the left corner and angle up 20 degrees to the right selvage edge. The very tip of the point of the material at the left bottom corner should be half way in the middle of the 1" masking tape. This strip of tape will be referred to as Tape I.

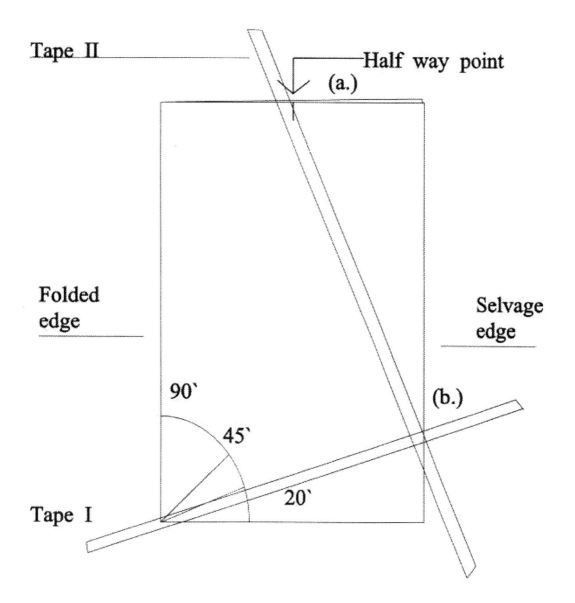

(a.) Find the half way point at the top of the folded material between the left folded edge and the selvage edge, make a small mark with a pencil or pen. Place a long strip of tape to the left of this mark so the right side of the tape is next to the mark.

(b.) Angle the tape down to meet where tape I ends on the right selvage edge. This will be referred to as Tape II.

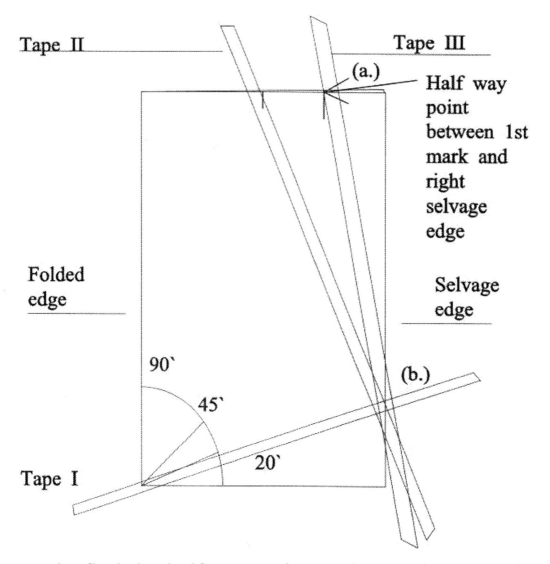

(a.) Again find the half way point at the top between the first mark made (at the right of Tape II) and the right selvage edge. Mark this spot with a pencil or pen. This time place a long strip of tape to the right of this mark so that the mark is on the left side of the tape.

(b.) Angle the tape down to meet where Tape I and Tape II end on the right selvage edge. This strip of tape will be referred to as Tape III.

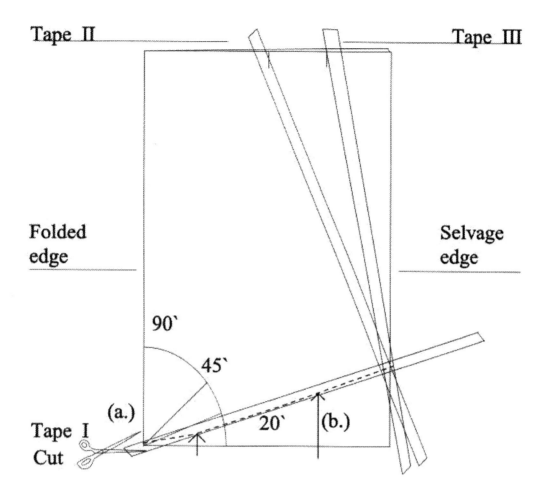

(a.) Tape I will be the guideline tape to make the bottom curve of the swag. Start at the left bottom corner of Tape I, and cut directly in the middle of the tape. Continue to cut in an absolute straight line. The tape will start to angle up but continue to cut straight until you meet the bottom edge of the tape.

(b.) At this point continue to cut along the bottom edge of the tape until you are half way across then gently start angling back up to the middle of the tape, and continue to cut in the middle of the tape until you reach the right selvage edge.

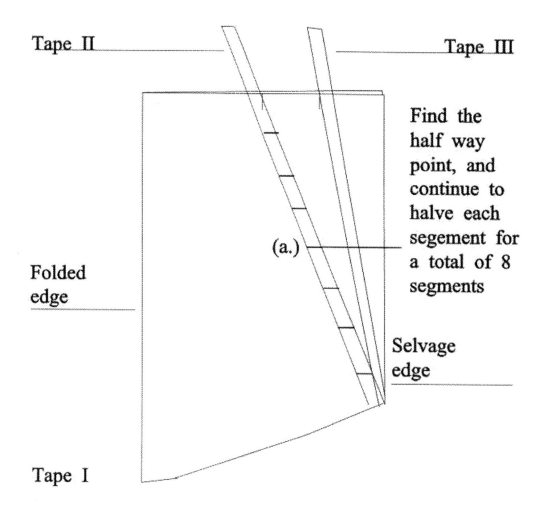

(a.) On Tape II make horizontal slash marks, with a pen, across the width of the tape from left to right. Find the halfway point of Tape II and make a horizontal slash mark, then again find the halfway point of each half. Continue to divide each segment in half until there 7 slash marks made, with a total of 8 segments. You may find a tape measure and calculator helpful to find the exact halfway points.

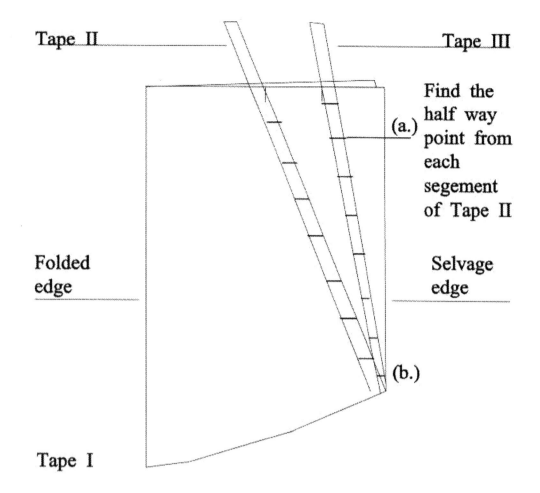

(a.) To mark Tape III, find the halfway point between each of the 7 slash marks on Tape II, at this point go directly over to Tape III and mark Tape III with a horizontal slash mark.

(b.) Do not forget the half way point between the 7th slash mark on Tape II and the very bottom edge of Tape II. There should be a total of 8 slash marks for Tape III.

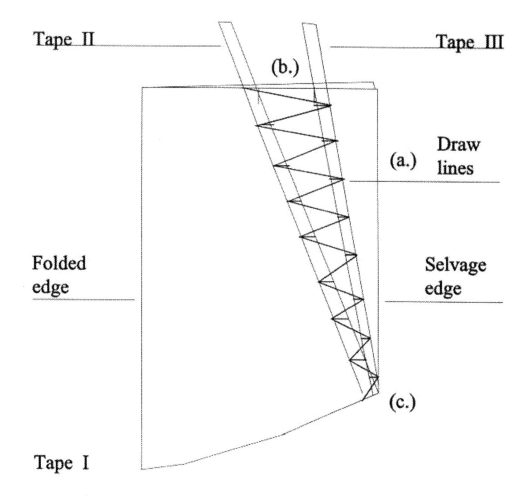

(a.) With a pen and ruler, or yardstick draw a straight line connecting the left side of the slash marks on Tape II to the right side of slash marks on Tape III.

(b.) These will be the cutting lines, after drawing these lines, go back and draw a line from the very top edge (left side) of Tape II to the first slash mark of Tape III (draw to the right side of slash mark of Tape III).

(c.) Also draw a line from the very bottom left edge of Tape II to the right of the last slash mark of Tape III. When cutting, do not cut this very last line drawn.

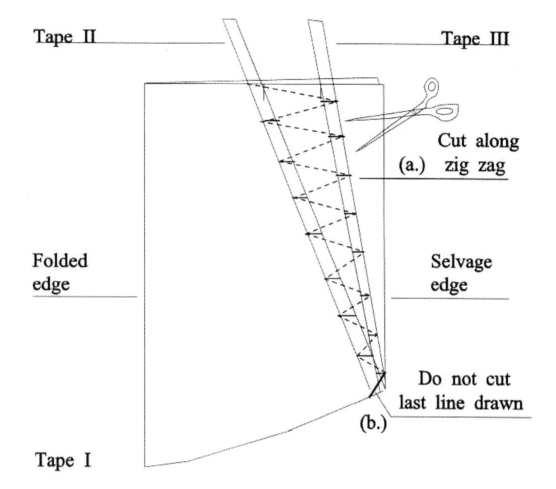

These drawn lines should form a zig zag where the indentations of the zig zag get deeper near the top.

(a.) Carefully cut along these drawn lines following the zig zag.

(b.) Except, do not cut the very last line drawn at the bottom of Tape II as this will make the last fold of the swag.

(a.) The pieces in between the zig zags should fall out, if not carefully remove them and carefully remove the tape.

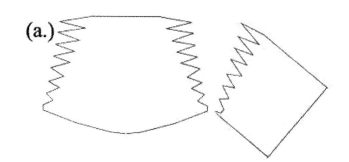

(b.) Unfold and pin the swag together as you would a finished swag.

(c.) Skip ahead to pages 187 to 190 in this chapter showing how to "pinch up the indentations" and "fold back the tails" to form the swag.

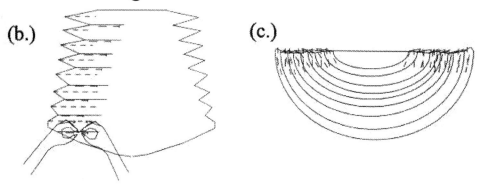

(d.) Lightly thumbtack it to the P.L. Strip* (see pages 195 and 196) and hold it up to the intended window to be treated. Judge if the size, etc. is satisfactory, make changes if needed at this point.

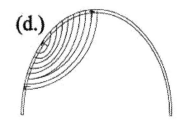

(e.) Unpin and fold the swag in half again to make changes so both sides will be even.

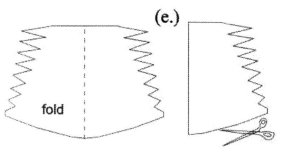

(a.) To cut the rest of the swags, first cut true squares (54" x 54") of both drapery and lining fabric (if swags are to be lined), for each swag. The squares will then be folded in half, selvage edge to selvage edge and the fold of the swag pattern will be placed on top of the fold of the squares.

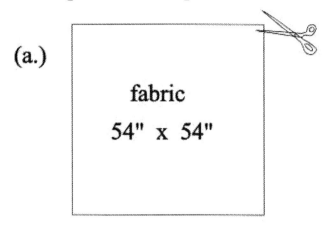

To cut a square first achieve a perfect straight line by

(b.) if the fabric is a cotton type fabric it may rip evenly along the woven threads however if the fabric is of a synthetic type material it may pull out of shape when attempting to rip it. If this is the case then see (b.) or (c.) on the following page.

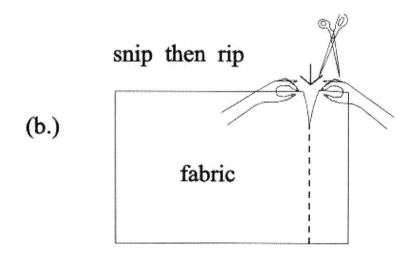

If the fabric pulls out of shape when trying to rip it then you will need to (b.) do it the harder way, the seamstress method.

The seamstress method involves pulling a thread and cutting along the line created by the pulled thread, to get a perfectly straight edge.

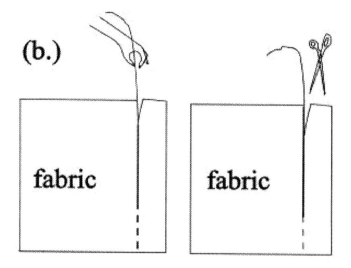

Or (c.) a roughly straight edge can be achieved by using a T-square and a strip of masking tape, fold the material in half from selvage edge to selvage edge and press, line up the T-square to the selvage edge and use masking tape to make a straight cutting line. After placing the masking tape, then go back and check both the folded edge and the selvage edge, to see if they line up with the T-square before cutting. Once certain then use the straight edge of the tape as the cutting guideline.

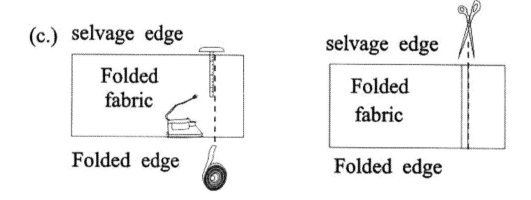

(a.) To make the rest of the swags from the pattern swag, place the fold of the pattern swag on top of the fold of the folded squares of drapery and lining fabric.

Ensure that the nap of the fabric runs in the same direction, and that the selvage edges are even.

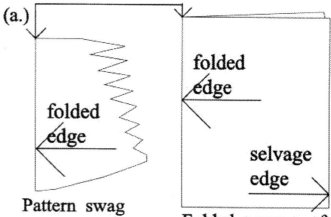

(b.) Pin in place and cut out along the top, bottom, and the zig zag side edges of the pattern swag

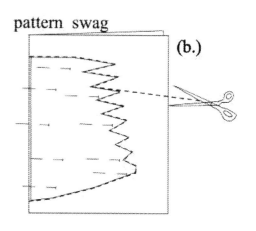

(c.) The pieces of material in between the zig zag should fall out. Carefully remove all pieces and separate the swags.

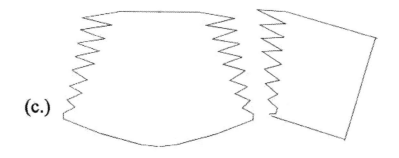

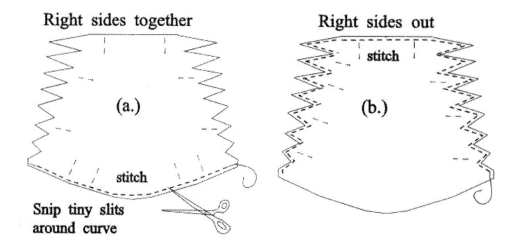

(a.) Unfold the material so the swags lay open and flat. If drapery lining was used then pair the drapery fabric and lining fabric right sides together and pin. Sew or Heat and Bond a 5/8" seam allowance to the bottom curve. Snip tiny slits around the curve, careful not to cut through the seam.

(b.) Iron seam of curve open and flat. Then turn swag back to right sides out, with wrong sides together, then press the seam to the lining side. Pin drapery and lining together, match up the zig zag, and stitch, or Heat and Bond a 5/8" seam allowance around the top and both sides of the zig zag. If no lining was used, then apply Fray Stop to all sides and the bottom curved edge. Then turn up bottom curved edge 1 /2" to 1 ", and apply Iron On Hem Binding Tape, or stitch in a hem.

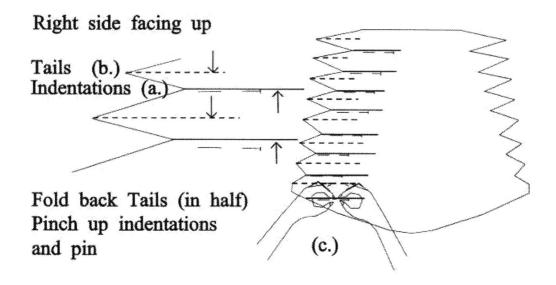

(a.) Where the zig zag formation goes in, will be referred to as the Indentations.

(b.) Where the zig zag goes out, will be referred to as the Tails. Starting with the left side of the swag pinch up and pin each of the Indentations. Insert straight pins to the underside of the pinch so that the point of the pin faces out and the head of the pin faces towards the middle of the swag.

Pinch up the Indentations so that the sides of the Tails of each Indentation line up even with each other.

(c.) The bottom (8th) fold of the swag is made by pinching up and pinning where you would imagine the next Indentation would be as it goes off the edge at the bottom.

Turn whole swag upside down, with right side facing up.

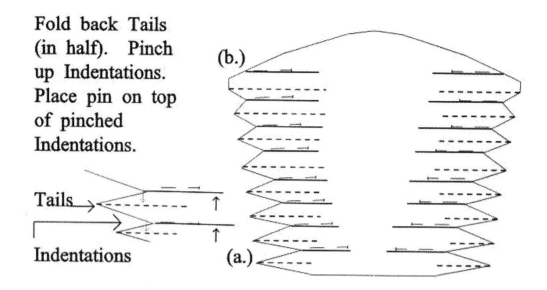

(a.) After pinching and pinning all of the Indentations on the left side of the swag, then turn the swag upside down and start from top to bottom pinching up and pinning Indentations on the remaining side. Again, insert the pin so that the point of the pin faces out and the head of the pin faces the middle of the swag. Also, be sure that when you pinch up and pin, that you place the pin on the same side of the pinch (this time on top instead of underneath) as you did on the other side of the swag. You will probably need to make a conscious effort to do this.

(b.) Also, remember to pinch up and pin the very last fold, where you would imagine the next Indentation would be as it goes off the edge of the bottom of the swag.

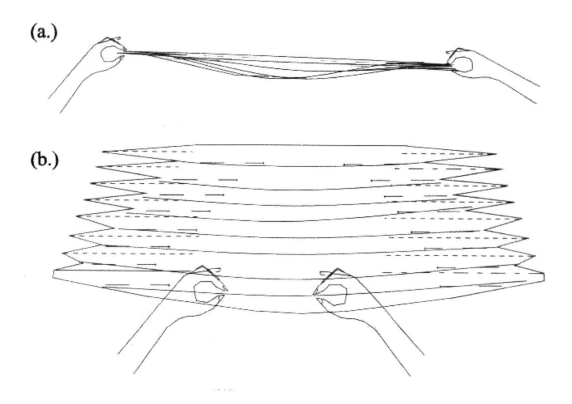

(a.) When finished pinching up and pinning all of the Indentations, then turn the swag back to the upright position. Pinch up and gather all the Indentations together, so that the Tails fold in half with the sides lined up evenly, then let them go. Then start again, this time more deliberate as directed below.

(b.) Start on the left side and work from top to bottom, finger press folds to the middle of the swag and then let it go. Do the same to the right side, except try to finger press folds across the swag to meet the folds on the otherside, then let it go. This is done so that the material will get the "idea" of how to "behave."

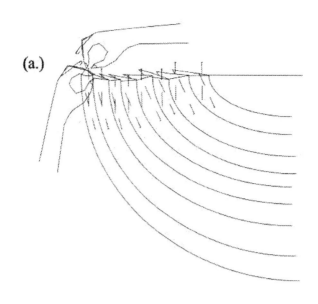

(a.) To form the swag, start at the top and work to the bottom, pinch up each pinned Indentation fold and bring it to the top straight edge of the swag and pin. Press the folds of the Tails flat and out to the side. When finished each of the folded Tails, and Indentations should line up straight across the top with each one a little farther out than the previous one.

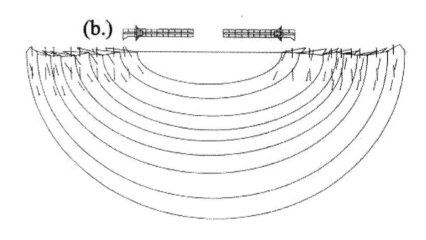

(b.) Use a sewing gauge to ensure the folds have been spaced the same distance on the right as the left.

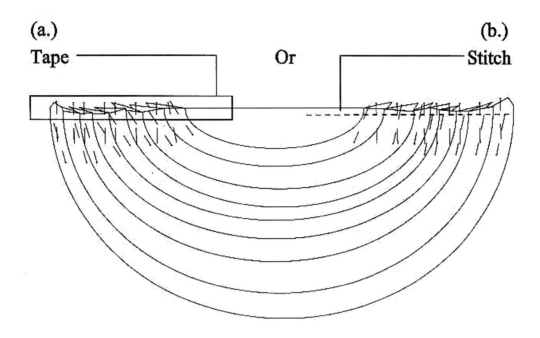

When folds are pulled up and complete you will need to secure the folds at the top.

(a.) If you are using the no sew method adjust folds evenly, and once the folds are adjusted and even then secure them with masking tape at the very top of the swag, then turn swag over and secure the back side of the folds with tape at the top. Leave the pins in place until the swag is secured to the P.L. Strip* with thumbtacks, then the pins can be removed.

(b.) If you are using the sewing method then secure the folds at the top with pins, then once certain both swags are as close to identical as possible, then straight stitch a 1/4" seam allowance across the top of the folds. After the folds are secured then remove the pins.

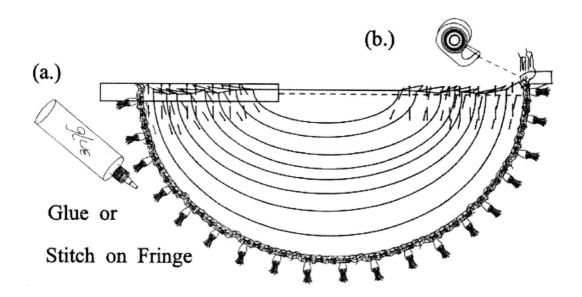

The bottom curve of the swag is finished. You may add fringe for added elegance, but it is not necessary.

(a.) If using fringe then apply it to the bottom edge of the swag with fabric glue or by stitching it in place. Fabric glue is recommended rather than hot glue, because it is much more forgiving, and this will be a highly visible area. To hold the fringe in place while the glue dries, use masking tape and or pins, but remove the tape or pins before the glue dries completely. Matching fringe is least likely to show imperfections.

(b.) Use clear Scotch tape on the ends of the fringe and leave in place to prevent the ends from unraveling.

Do all of the above to the second swag which is the other half of the curtain. Try to make them exactly alike.

Overall View

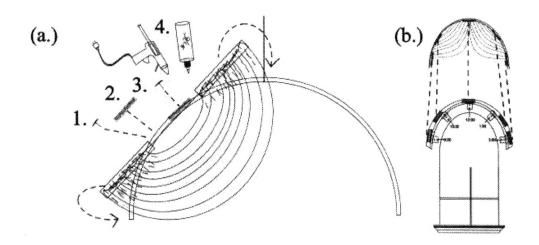

Each one of the swags will hang on half of the curtain, and this is how your swags will be applied to the P.L. Strip*, which then is then attached to the P.M.M. Board* and held in place by velcro. The swags will be applied to one side of the P.L. Strip* with

(a.) (a.1.) thumbtacks and then on top of that the (a.2.) velcro will then be applied over the thumbtacks, then the velcro will be secured with more (a.3.) thumbtacks. Later when satisfied with how the swags are positioned, then the velcro can be reinforced with (a.4.) fabric glue or hot glue.

(b.) As the velcro side is turned over and placed down to marry with the velcro on the P.M.M. Board*, the thumbtacks, tape, and velcro will all be hidden underneath. Only the graceful folds of the swag flowing over the P.M.M. Board* will be visible. The following pages give a more detailed description of how to apply the swags to the P.L. Strip*.

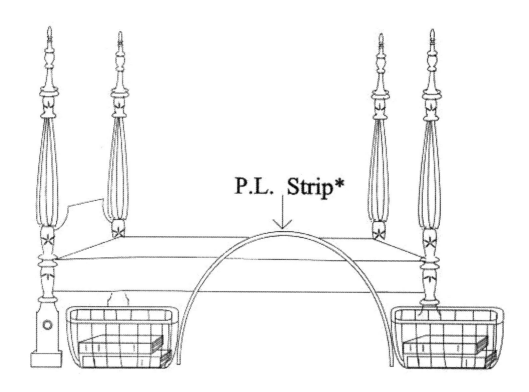

A good place to work with your P.L. Strip* and swag is next to a bed or table, where it can lean and stand upright in a curved form position. Use 2 objects to keep the ends of the P.L. Strip* from slipping away. One example could be 2 laundry baskets with clothes or books in them for weight. Approximate the width of the window and place the laundry baskets that far apart next to the bed or table. Bend the P.L. Strip* so each end rests on the carpet against the laundry baskets. Let the P.L. Strip* lean against the bed or table. This will keep it in a upright position. You will need to work with the P.L. Strip* bent in the upright position because in this position you can approximate the curve of your window. If you try and work with the P.L. Strip* flat all the time it will be harder to see how the curtain is likely to hang.

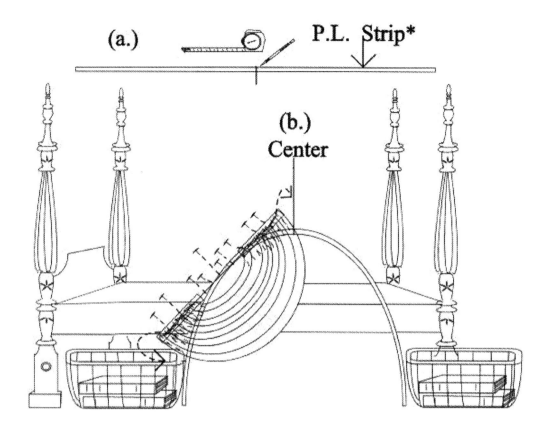

(a.) First find and mark the center of the P.L. Strip*. Do this by measuring the entire length to the nearest 1 /8" and then divide this number by 2. A calculator can be helpful when dividing fractions of an inch (0.5 = 1 /2" etc.) or use the metric side of the tape measure, if there is one. First start on the left side of the P.L. Strip*, for the left half of the swag curtain.

(b.) The right edge of the left sided swag will be the middle of the whole curtain, place it a little past the center. The right and left ends (at the top) of the swag will need to hang over the P.L. Strip* by 2" to 3" but the middle of the swag will barley cover the edge, so when the P.L. Strip* is in the half round curved form, the swag will conform to this shape. Secure the swag to the P.L. Strip* with short thumbtacks.

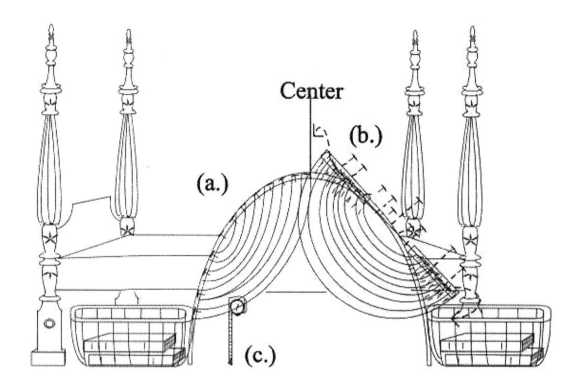

(a.) Be sure the folds lay flat and the swag hangs nicely, and that there is an overlap at the center, readjust as needed. Be sure to use short thumbtacks. Place a thumbtack at least every other fold or at every fold if necessary and place 2 to 3 thumbtacks in the middle of the swag. If you have used the no sew method and left the straight pins in for added support to the masking tape, then remove them after the swag has been adequately secured to the P.L. Strip* with the thumbtacks, and after putting the swag through a dry test run.

(b.) Repeat the same process for the other side (the right half of the curtain) only vice versa. Be sure to over lap at the center.

(c.) Ensure the bottom ends of the swags are even, the same distance from the ends of the P.L. Strip*.

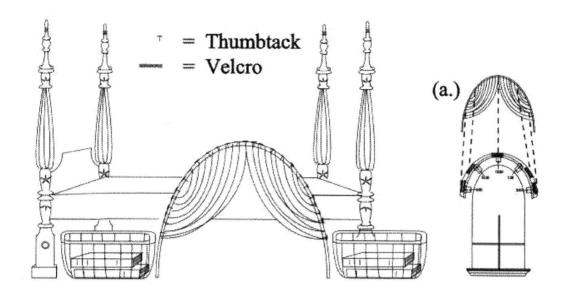

(a.) At this point it is a good idea to put the swag through a "dry test run", to see how the swags look laying on top of the P.M.M. Board*. Turn the swags over with the thumbtack side of the P.L. Strip* down, as it will be when marrying the velcroed side down to the P.M.M. Board*.

Be sure the two halves of the swag over lap each other enough to cover the hardware underneath. Also be sure the two halves of the swag over lap enough, so that all or most of the sheet rock surrounding the window is covered, and the the divide of the swags should come down to a point near the level of the glass of the window. Readjust as needed. Temporarily hold the swaged P.L. Strip* in place by slipping a strip of masking tape in the small gap between the P.M.M. Board* and the wall, to wrap around the end of the P.L. Strip* and the P.M.M. Board*, see page 200 (c.).

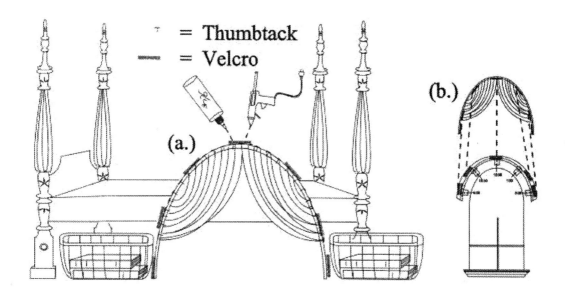

(a.) Once satisfied with how both of the swags look and hang, then place strips of velcro over the thumbtacks at 12:00, 1:30, 10:30, 3:00, 9:00 and at the very ends. Then secure the velcro with more thumbtacks and fabric glue or hot glue. (b.) The velcro side will be turned over and placed down to marry with the velcro at the same clock positions on the velcro to the back of the P.M.M. Board*.

As the following pages detail, the drapery panel treatment, "Rod Pocket Sleeve Drapery Panels With Diagonal Cut To Fit Arched Windows", will need to have double strips of velcro placed across the P.M.M. Board* at each of the clock positions and at the very ends. For the drapery panel treatment, "Two Short Side Boards Drapery Panels", only single strips of velcro at the back of each of the clock positions and the very ends will be needed.

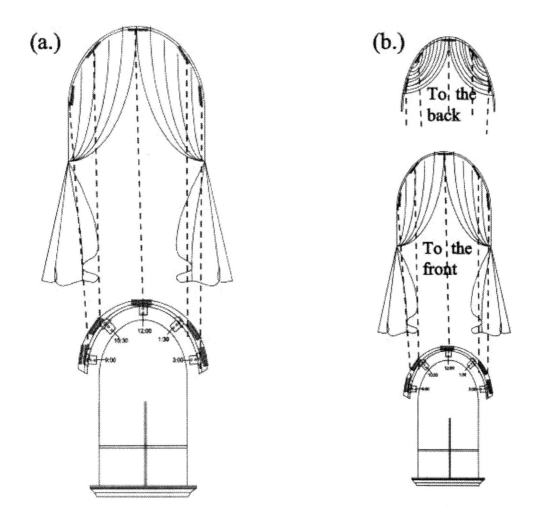

(a.) Double strips of velcro are placed on the P.M.M. Board* at each or the clock positions and at the very ends, across the width of the P.M.M. Board*. The velcro on the front half of the P.M.M. Board* will marry to the velcro of the P.L. Strip* of the diagonal cut drapery panels. Line up the centers.

(b.) The swags will lay over the drapery panels and the velcro of the swaged P.L. Strip* will marry to the velcro on the back of the P.M.M. Board*, behind the drapery panels. Be sure all the centers line up, or at least appear centered.

Since the under drapery panels are in front of the swags, there will be a small space left showing the swaged P.L. Strip* and the P.M.M. Board*.

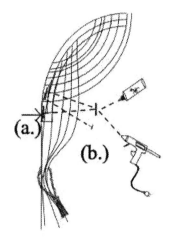

(a.) To correct this apply small strips of velcro or thumbtacks to marry both the edge of the drapery panel to the P.L. Strip* of the top treatment.

(b.) Place the velcro on the wrong side of of the drapery panel along the side hem line. Start placing the marrying velcro up under the top treatment and continue as needed untill the panel flows down the side of the P.M.M. Board* evenly. Spot weld marrying velcro or thumbtack any spots as needed.

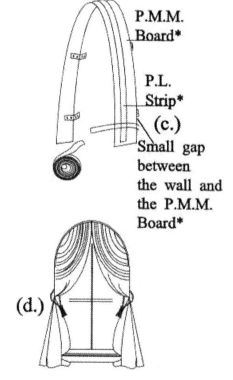

(c.) To secure the very end of the P.L. Strip* to the end of the P.M.M. Board*, slip a strip of 1" masking tape up in the small gap between the wall and the P.M.M. Board*. Wrap the tape completely around the two ends. Here it is shown illustrated without the drapery treatment, but do this after the drapery treatment has been applied.

(d.) Stand back and evaluate for symmetry, readjust as needed. Add tie backs for a finished and polished look.

(a.) To apply the top swaged P.L. Strip* to the "Two Short Side Boards Drapery Panels", apply the short side boards first as directed in chapter 6. Be sure the outer sides of the panels will be able to go around the P.M.M. Board* and lay flat against it, and that the swags will hang down far enough to cover the short side boards.

(b.) Place the swaged P.L. Strip* so it will marry to the velcro at the back of the P.M.M. Board*. At the sides, apply small strips of velcro to marry the outer edge of the drapery panel, to the slot which is under the swags, but on top of the P.L. Strip* that the swags are on, so all that shows are the swags laying on top of the drapery panels.

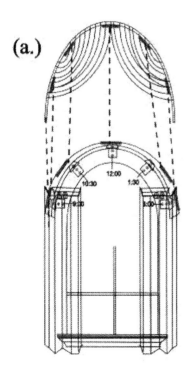

(a.)

Apply small strips of velcro to marry the outer edge of the drapery panel, to the slot which is under the swags, but on top of the P.L. Strip*

(b.)

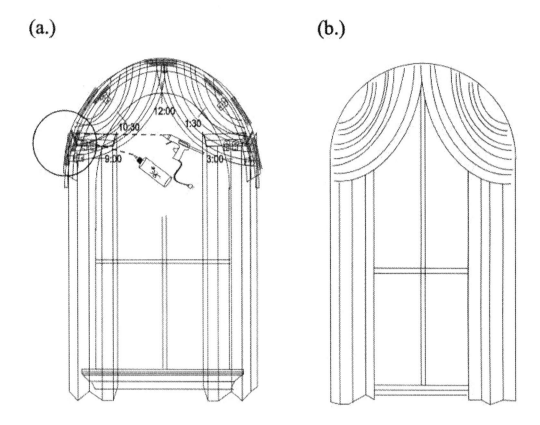

(a.) Stand back and evaluate for symmetry, make adjustments as necessary. When satisfied with the placements of the velcro and how the side panels lay etc., then go back and reinforce the velcro with hot glue or fabric glue.

(b.) For this window treatment tie backs are not needed. For privacy add sheers and or miniblinds.

Chapter 9
Single Swag

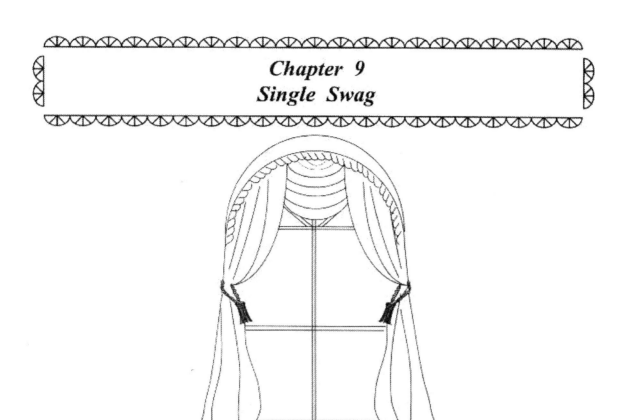

The "Single Swag" is placed under a "Covered Jute Webbing" and the "Rod Pocket Sleeve Drapery Panel With A Diagonal Cut to Fit Arched Windows". This is done by using a single swag that is mounted on a P.L. Strip* which is attached to the front of the P.M.M. Board*. Over that the "Rod Pocket Sleeve Drapery Panel With A Diagonal Cut" is applied to the P.L. Strip* and attached to the back of the P.M.M. Board*. Over both of these the "Covered Jute Webbing" is applied and secured by velcro.

* Polystyrene Lattice Strip abbreviated as P.L. Strip*
* Polystyrene Moulding Mounting Board abbreviated as P.M.M. Board*

Checklist For Tools and Supplies

* Drapery fabric
* Drapery lining
* 2 P.L. Strips*
* Velcro
* Swag pattern
* Directions for chapter 5 "Rod Pocket Sleeve Drapery Panels With a Diagonal Cut to Fit Arched Windows"
* Directions for "Covered Jute Webbing" page 67 (found as the top treatment in chapter 4 "No Sew Gathered Sheet Drapes"
* Directions for chapter 7 "Outside Mount Triple Swag"
* Matching thread or 1 roll of Heat and Bond
* 2 Tassled tie back holders
* Sissors
* Iron and Steam iron
* Tape measure
* Dissappearing ink pen (optional) or Dressmakers chalk
* 2 Cup hooks or nails
* Fabric glue
* Hot glue
* Jute Webbing (yardage = length of P.M.M. Board* from 3" to 6" past the 3:00 to 9:00 o'clock position)
* Cording trim with webbed edge yardage = same as above + 6")
* 1 & 1/2 yards of Heat and Bond off the bolt
* 1" Masking tape
* String

Drapery and Lining Fabric Yardage Estimation

"Covered Jute Webbing" = same length of P.M.M. board* (from 3" to 6" past the 3:00 and 9:00 o'clock position)

+

"Single Swag", estimate 2 yards

+

Drapery Panels, see yardage estimation page 93 in chapter 5 "Rod Pocket Sleeve Drapery Panels with Diagonal Cut to Fit Arched Windows"

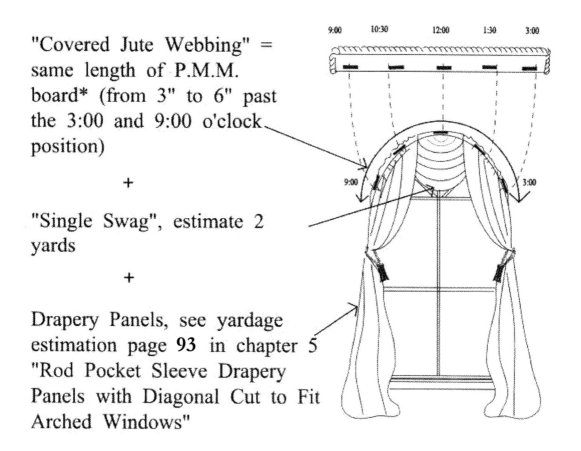

Combine the yardage for the "Covered Jute Webbing" plus the yardage for the "Single Swag" plus the yardage for the "Rod Pocket Sleeve Drapery Panels" for each, the drapery fabric and lining fabric yardage. To get the "yardage" figure divide the total number of inches by 36, and round up to the next 1/4 yard to know what to tell your fabric store sales person. Any swag pattern can be used however it is recommended to make a test swag to determine appropriate size swag for the window size.

The following directions are a shorten version of the swag application as outlined in the chapter 7 "Outside Mount Triple Swag". The "Single Swag" will have only one swag applied to the middle of the P.L. Strip*. Refer to the above named chapter for additional explanation in how to mount the swag etc.

To make the "Single Swag" window treatment, firstmake a swag. Most any swag pattern will do, or the swag pattern in this book, chapter 8 "Half Dimension Swags" pages 172 to 192, can be used except make the swag smaller by using a smaller square 48" x 48", or any size square depending on your window size. The 54" x 54" square makes a very large swag. Cut out atrial swag out of inexpensive muslin or old bed sheet, to test for size and uniformity, make adjustments as needed. A store bought ready made swag can even be used, making minor adjustments.

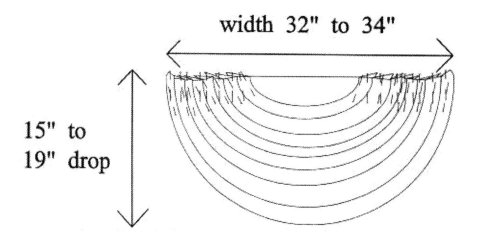

Most any swag pattern will do. The swag should have a 15" to 19" drop, and 32" to 34" width, depending on the window size.

(a.) If the swags are large enough then they can be directly applied to the

(b.) P.L. Strip* and held in place with thumbtacks.

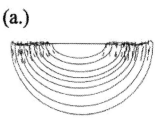
(a.)

(b.)

1 = Thumbtack
2 = Velcro
3 = P.L. Strip*

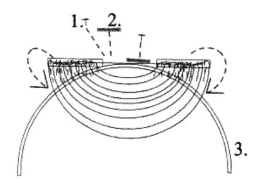

(c.) However in many cases with a swag pattern the addition of a tab to the top of the swag will be needed to allow for more working room with the middle of the swag when it is applied to the P.L. Strip*. If a tab to the swag is needed then first make the swag and then refer to pages 139 to 142 (a.) to make the tab.

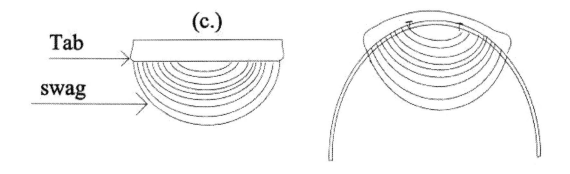

Mount the single swag to the middle of the P.L. Strip* using the "Swag Lattice Turned Over" method. Below is a quick over view, refer to the listed page numbers for a more detailed explanation, using only the one swag at the center of the P.L. Strip*.

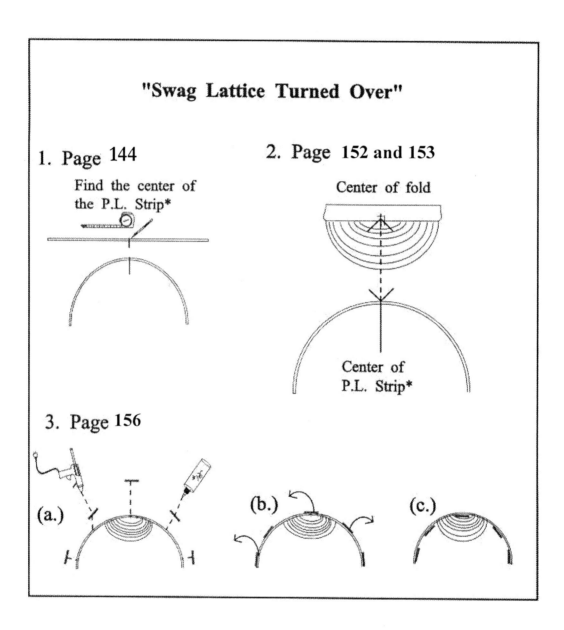

(a.) The velcro of the "Single Swag" (a.) P.L. Strip* will marry to the velcro at the front edge of the P.M.M. Board*.

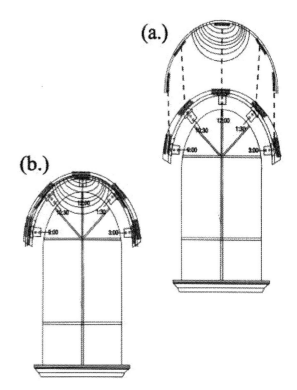

(b.) With the "Single Swag" finding the exact middle will not be as critical as it is with the triple swag because with the "Single Swag" the P.L. Strip* can be moved independently if needed, to line up the exact center.

(c.) Make the drapery panel treatment the "Rod Pocket Sleeve Drapery Panels With a Diagonal Cut To Fit Fit Arched Windows" as directed in chapter 5 pages 91 to 112. Apply the drapery panels to the P.L. Strip* and adjust the panels so that they do not meet at the top and that the top of the P.L. Strip* is left open as shown on page 107 (c.). Apply a few short thumbtacks to stabilize the sleeve so it does not tend to slip off the P.L. Strip*.

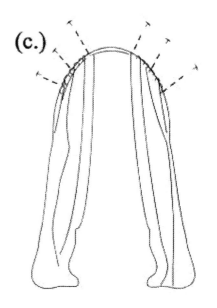

(a.) Apply velcro on the underneath side of the "Rod Pocket Sleeve Drapery Panel" P.L. Strip*, with hot glue or fabric glue, at 12:00, 1:30, 10:30, 3:00, 9:00 o'clock and at the very ends, and any other areas needed.

(b.) Apply the P.L. Strip* with the "Rod Pocket Sleeve Drapery Panel" over the "Single Swag" and attach it to the velcro at the back edge of the P.M.M. board*.

(c.) Arrange the folds of the swag and panels so they lay smooth and even.

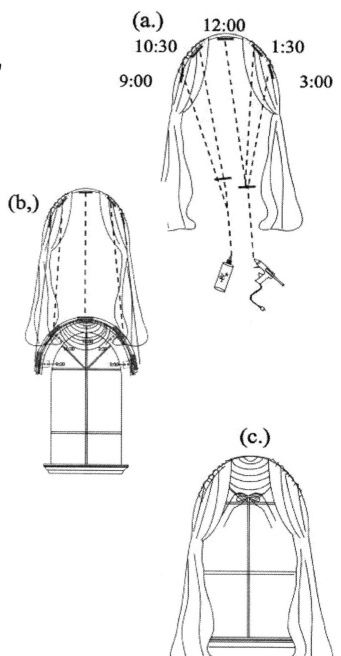

(a.) The Covered Jute Webbing will cover up the bare P.L. Strip* and will provide a smooth neat covering for this window treatment. Follow the general outline in the section "Covered Jute Webbing", pages 67 to 75, in chapter 4 "No Sew Gathered Sheet Drapes". Also the "Simply Covered Crinoline" as outlined in the same chapter, on pages 79 to 84, will work nicely with this window treatment.

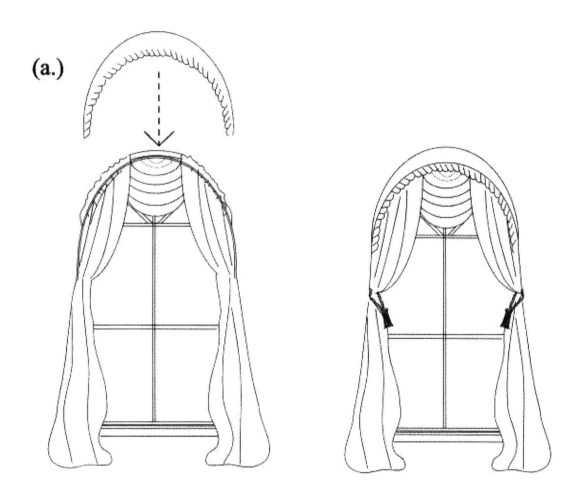

The directions on the following pages detail the application of the cover to the "Single Swag" window treatment.

(a.) Apply 2 rows of 4" to 6" strips of velcro to the underside of the "Covered Jute Webbing" at the middle and towards the back edge. Place these rows at 12:00, 1:30, 10:30, 3:00, 9:00, and at the very ends if needed, and any other places needed.

(b.) Also apply 2 rows of the 4" to 6" strips of velcro at the same positions in the middle and towards the back on top of the "Rod Pocket Sleeve Drapery Panels with a Diagonal Cut To Fit Arched Windows".

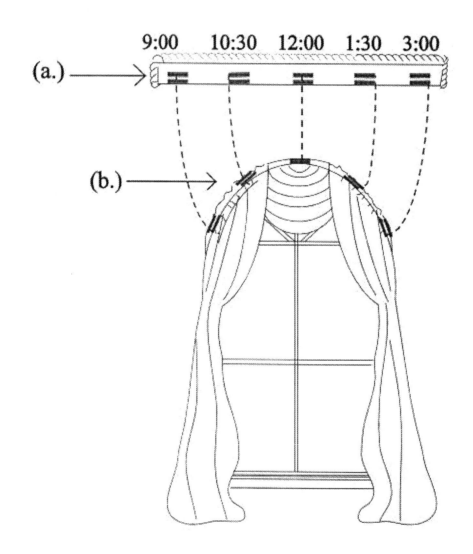

After the positions of the velcro have been established, and you are satisfied with how they look, then go back and apply fabric glue or hot glue under the velcro to provide extra adhesion. If you are uncertain of your abilities to handle a hot glue gun while up on a ladder, then use the fabric glue and wait 24 hours for it to dry. See page 110 (a.), (b.), and (c.) to finish the sides of the drapery panels and to secure the P.L. Strip to the P.M.M. Board*.

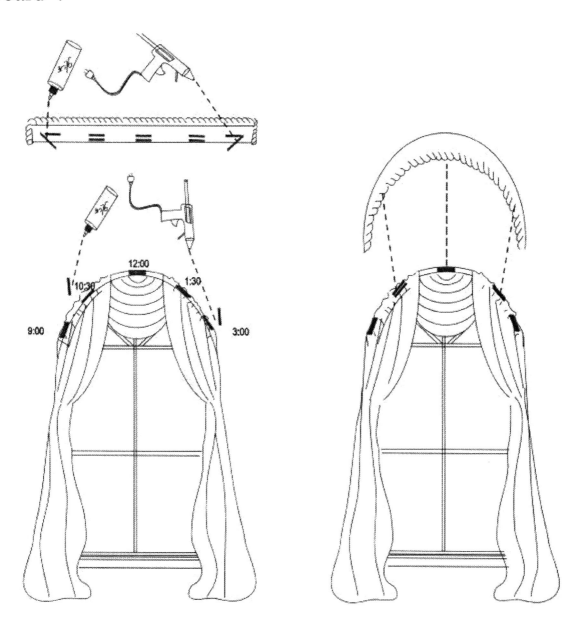

Use cuphooks or nails to hold back the tie backs to the side of the drapery panels. With the "Single Swag" window treatment, the tie backs are placed much higher in the window treatment. This is done so that most of the swag will be visible. Below shows the comparison where tie backs are placed in the window treatment "Outside Mount Triple Swag" as compared to where they are placed in the "Single Swag".

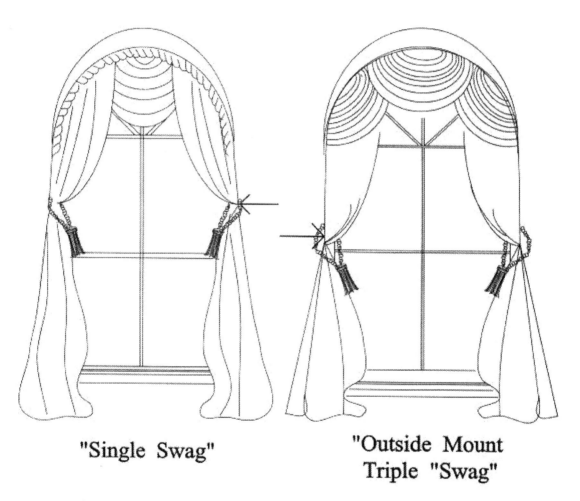

"Single Swag"   "Outside Mount Triple "Swag"

Place the tie backs much higher in the "Single Swag".

Chapter 10
Simple No Sew Drapes with Brass Tie Backs

This simple "Outside Mount" window treatment involves one long piece of drapery fabric and lining. Skinny barely seen tie backs are used to hold back most of the fabric, while decorative brass tie backs are used for a striking appearance. This will be a stationary window treatment.

* Polystyrene Lattice Strip abbreviated as P.L. Strip*
* Polystyrene Moulding Mounting Board abbreviated as P.M.M. Board*

Checklist for Tools and Supplies

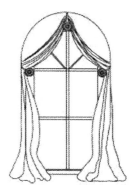

* Drapery fabric
* Drapery lining
* 3 Decorative brass tie backs (or any kind of hard decorative tie backs)
* Sissors
* 2 rolls of 3/4" Heat and Bond
* 1 1/2 yards of Heat and Bond off the bolt
* Short thumbtacks
* Masking tape
* String
* Hot glue gun
* Velcro
* Dissappearing ink pen
* Jute Webbing length = length of P.M.M. Board*
* Crinoline length = length same as Jute Webbing
* Quilt batting
* Large safety pins or
* Needle and matching thread to whipstitch
* Directions for the "Outside Mount"

Since one piece of fabric is used, try to purchase fabric without an obvious directional print, it would show the fabric print going up on one side and down on the other. A solid color would be an excellent choice.

The next page shows how to measure for the drapery fabric and lining.

Drapery and Lining Yardage Estimation

(a.) (This measurement + 36")
x 2 = lining fabric yardage, add 3" more to this figure for drapery fabric yardage

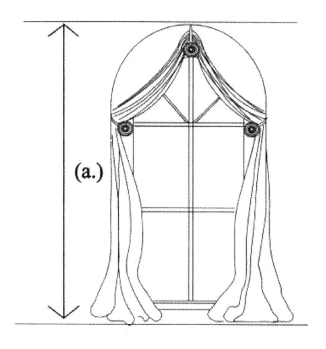

Measure from the top of the arch to the floor add 36", for puddles, swags, and trim off allowance then double this figure for there to enough fabric to go up and down both sides of the window. This will be the exact amount needed for the lining fabric. Add 3" more to this figure for the amount needed for the drapery fabric. These extra 3" of drapery fabric will be used to make the skinny tiebacks. To get the "yardage" figure, divide the number of inches by 36, and round up to the next 1/4 of yard to know what to tell your fabric store sales person.

The base, which to attach the drapery panel to the P.M.M. Board*, is made of the Jute Webbing, Crinoline, and Quilt Batting.

Use the measurements obtained on page 217 to make the drapery panel. Cut 3" off of one end of the drapery fabric, for the tie backs, then cut each the drapery and lining fabric one long piece, the length of the measurement from the top of the arch to the floor plus 36" x 2.

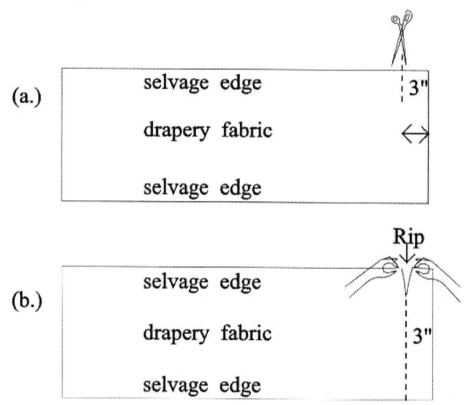

Cut off 3" from the end (from selvage edge to selvage edge) of the drapery fabric. If the drapery fabric rips easily without pulling out of shape, then rip the fabric so it will tear along a straight line.

(a.) Make a small cut with scissors on one selvage edge then

(b.) rip smartly, the material should tear evenly, as evidenced by being able to pull a single thread on the end from selvage edge to selvage edge.

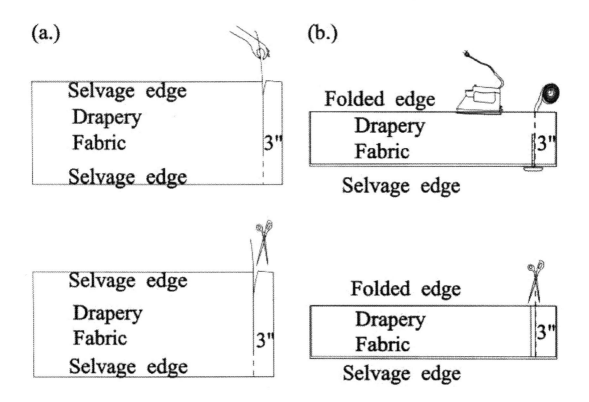

(a.) If the drapery fabric pulls out of shape and gets cattywompas when you rip it, then you will need to do it the harder way by pulling a thread and cut along the line created by the pulled thread, to get a perfectly straight edge.

(b.) A roughly straight edge can be achieved by using a T-square and a strip of masking tape as a cutting guide. Fold the material in half from selvage edge to selvage edge, ensure evenous and then iron the folded side. Line up the T-square to the selvage edge and folded edge and use the straight edge of the masking tape as a cutting guide.

(a.) To make the skinny tie backs first cut the 3" strip of Drapery fabric into 3 equal pieces, each approximately 18" long by 3" wide.

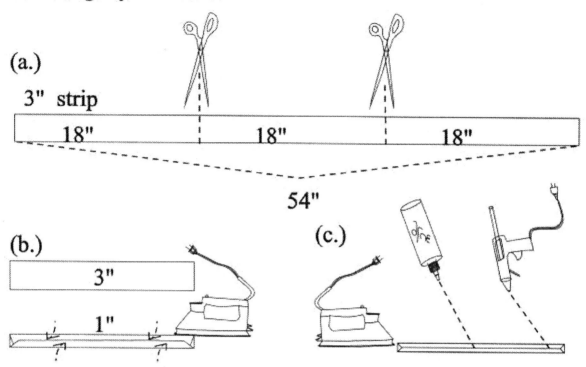

(b.) Fold the strips 1" wide lengthwise, so the seam is hidden in the middle of the back, then it iron flat.

(c.) Use Heat and Bond, fabric glue, or hot glue to tack down the strips to form the skinny tie backs. Keep the skinny tieback as flat and smooth as possible, so they can slip in the small gap between the wall and the P.M.M. Board*. If you are using the hot glue, press it down so there are not any large lumps of glue. TIP: Use a piece of masking tape that has been doubled on itself to shield your fingers from the heat. If you are using the fabric glue, press the strips between wax paper and books to flatten and wait 24 hours to dry.

(a.) To make the lined drapery panel first ensure that each end of the drapery fabric is straight, by methods described earlier (cut and rip, cutting along a pulled thread, or T-square). Pair the drapery and lining fabric together, and use the straight edge of the drapery fabric to cut the lining fabric even with the drapery fabric.

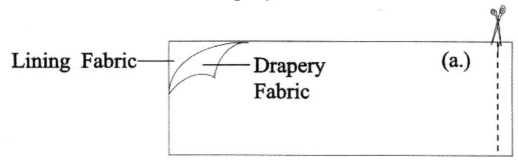

(b.) Then find the middle of the lining fabric by folding the material in half. Use a small piece of masking tape or pins to mark the fold.

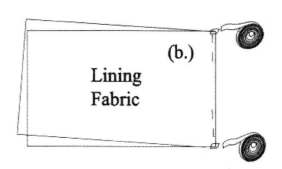

(c.) Place a long strip of 1" masking tape across the middle of the lining fabric, on the right side of the fabric. This strip of tape should stretch across from selvage edge to selvage edge. This will denote the middle, for later reference with the Jute Webbing and Crinoline.

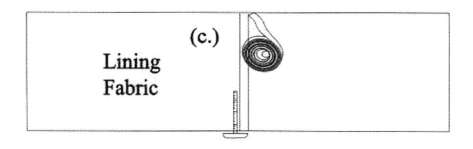

(a.) Remove small pieces of the outside edges of the tape that denotes the middle of the lining fabric, so it does not get caught up in the side seam.

(a.)

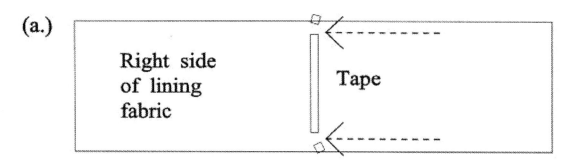

(b.) Pair up the drapery fabric with the lining fabric right sides together and pin. The edges of the tape have been removed so they do not get caught up in the side seams. With right sides together, Heat and Bond (or if preferred stitch a 5/8" seam allowance being sure to include the selvage edges) only on the side seams of drapery and lining fabric, leaving the ends open. The tape that denotes the middle will be on the inside, and will be visible when the panel is turned right side out.

(b.)

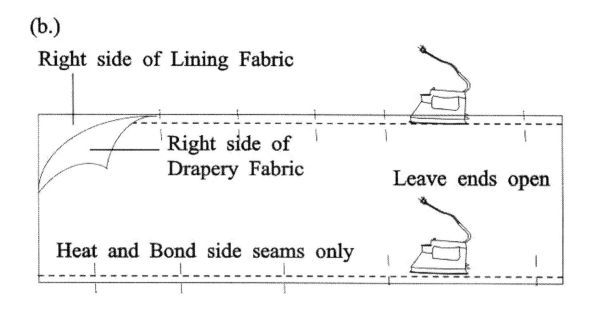

(a.) Through the open end, turn the panel right side out. Iron a crease in the seam to the lining side.

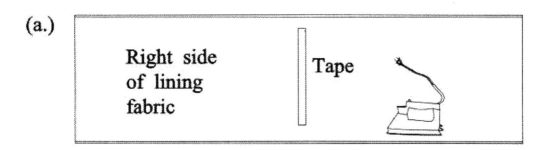

(b.) To finish the ends of the drapery panel, turn the raw edges of each, the lining and drapery fabric in 1 /2" towards the inside of the drapery panel. Iron flat first then, slip a strip of the Heat and Bond in between them, and bond them together (or if preferred stitch).

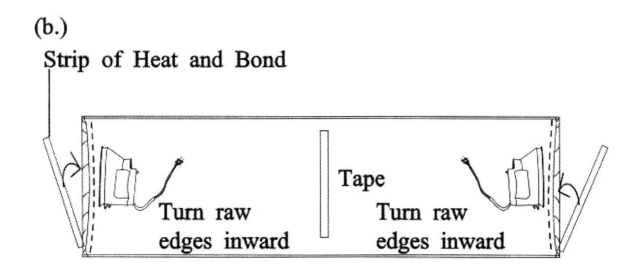

To make the base for the drapery panel to attach to the P.M.M. Board*, measure the entire arch, from the 3:00 to the 9:00 o'clock positions. (a.) Use a long piece of string and 3 pieces of masking tape. Tape the approximate middle of the string and place it at the 12:00 o'clock position on the arch. (b.) Allow the string to flow down along the arch of the board to the 3:00 and 9:00 o'clock positions and mark these each with another piece of tape, just below the corner iron. Cut the string the length of the P.M.M.Board*. (c.) Remove the string with the 3:00, 9:00, and 12:00 o'clock pieces of tape left on the string.

This string and the taped markings will be used as reference points for the base, made of the Jute Webbing, Crinoline, and Quilt Batting.

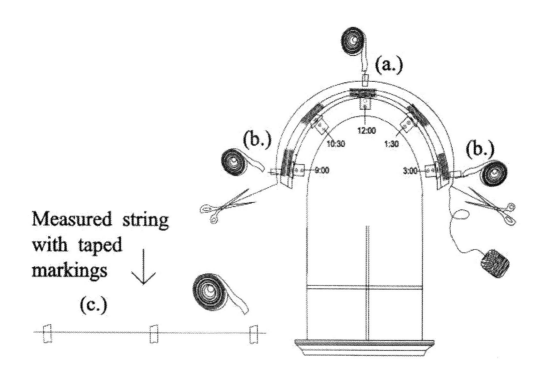

(a.) Cut the Jute Webbing the length of the measured string.

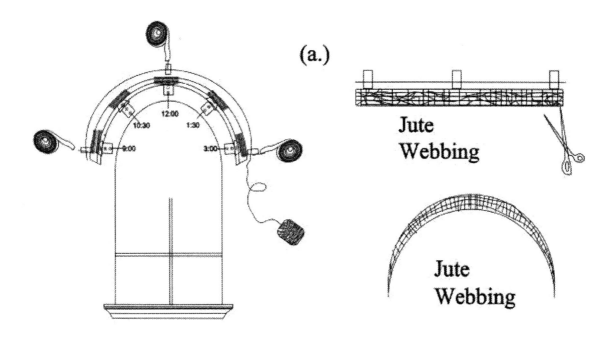

(b.) Iron strips of Heat and Bond to the Jute Webbing. Use the Heat and Bond that comes off the bolt, then cut strips to fit the Jute Webbing, and iron it onto the Jute Webbing.

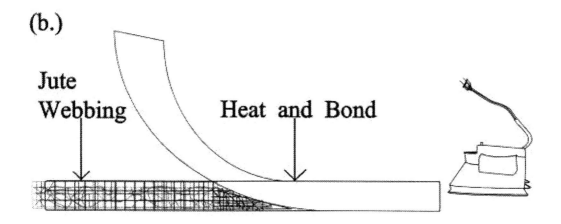

(a.) If using the P.M.M. Board* size 1/2" x 3 1/4" then the width of the Jute Webbing will be fine. However if the P.M.M. Board* size 1/2" x 2 7/16" was used then the Jute Webbing will need to be trimmed. Trim both, the Jute Webbing with the ironed on Heat and Bond, to the size of the width of the P.M.M. Board*. Trimming after the Heat and Bond has been applied causes less fraying of the Jute Webbing.

(a.)

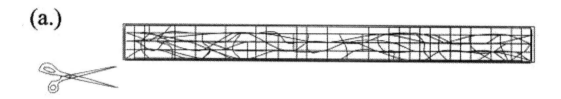

(b.) Heat and Bond the Jute Webbing to the Crinoline, trim if needed. The Jute webbing will be velcroed down to the P.M.M. Board*, and the Crinoline will be on top of the Jute Webbing. The next layer on top of the Crinoline will be the Quilt Batting.

(b.)

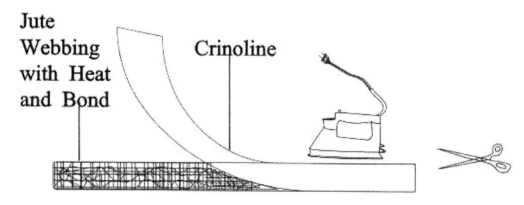

(a.) Trim the length of the Quilt Batting to be the length of the Jute Webbing and Crinoline. Trim the width to be approximately 8".

(a.)

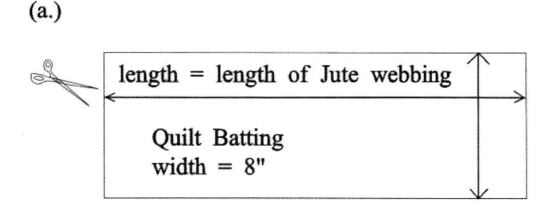

(b.) Fold the Quilt Batting in half length wise so it will be doubled layered. It will lie double layered on top of the Crinoline.

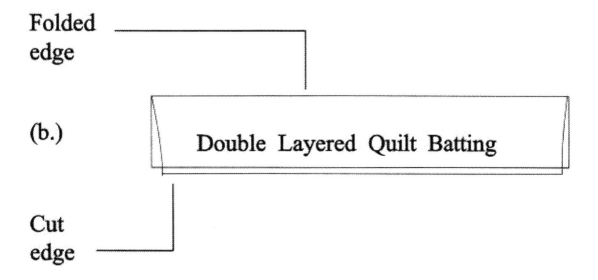

(a.) Place the double layered Quilt Batting flat. Place the Heat and Bonded Jute Webbing and Crinoline down on the Quilt Batting, with the Crinoline next to the Quilt Batting, 1" from the cut edge of the of the Quilt Batting.

(a.)

Place 1" from the cut edge of the Quilt Batting

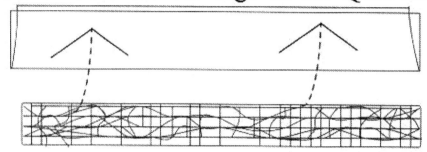

(b.) Fold both of the 1" cut edges of Quilt Batting over the Jute webbing and glue both edges in place onto the under side of the Jute webbing. Use Fabric glue or Hot glue.

Fold and glue both of the cut edges of the Quilt Batting over the Jute Webbing

(b.)

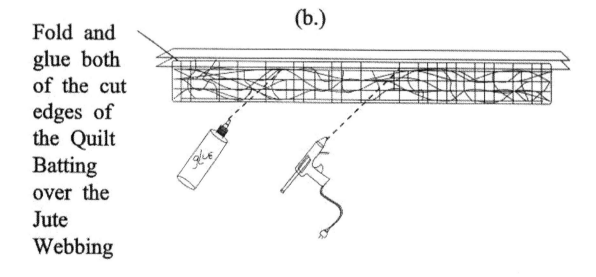

(a.) Using the marked taped string as a guide line up the middle of the Jute Webbing with the Crinoline and Quilt Batting to the middle of the lining side of the Lined Drapery Panel.

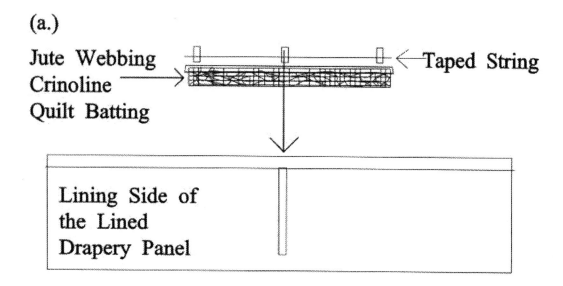

(b.) Place the middle of the Jute Webbing on top of the middle of the Lined Drapery Panel. With the under side of the Jute Webbing facing up, place the Jute Webbing, with the Crinoline and Quilt Batting side down on the lining side of the Line Drapery Panel. When the middles are lined up scoot the Jute Webbing back 1" to 1 1/2".

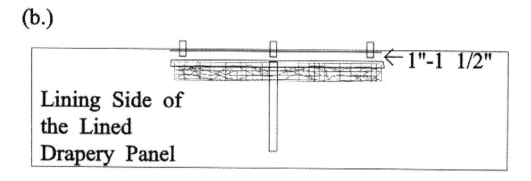

(a.) Fold the edge of the Lined Drapery Panel over the Jute Webbing. This side of the Jute Webbing will lay flat against the P.M.M. Board*, with the edge next to the wall, the Lined Drapery Panel will drape over the front of the P.M.M. Board*.

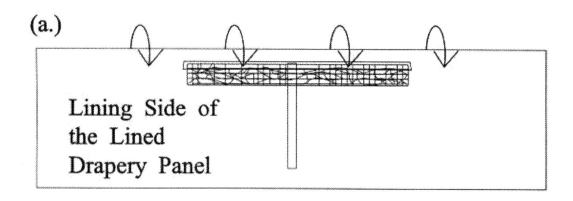

(b.) After folding the edge of the Lined Drapery Panel over the Jute Webbing, then secure it with Hot glue, Fabric glue, or Heat and Bond. As stated this folded side of the Lined Drapery Panel will be placed down on the P.M.M. Board*, next to the wall.

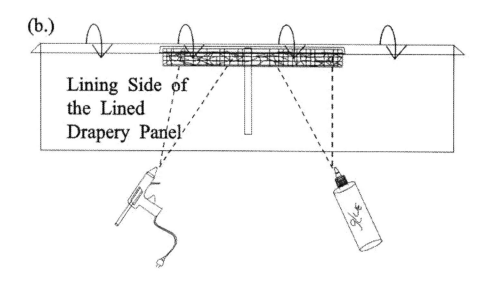

After you have folded the edge of the Lined Drapery Panel over the Jute Webbing, and have tacked down the edge with gule, or Heat and Bond, then apply velcro on top of this glued down edge and to the Jute Webbing.

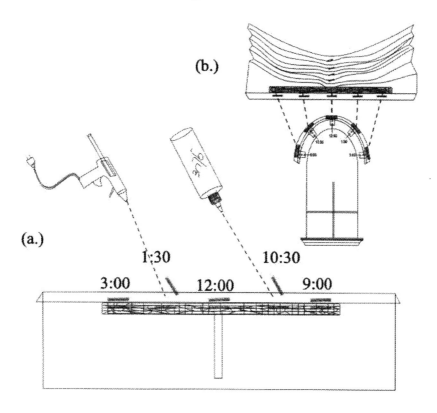

(a.) Place 2 rows of 4" to 6" strips of velcro to match the velcro in place on the outside mount of the P.M.M. Board*. Place these at 12:00, 1:30, 10:30, 3:00, and 9:00 o'clock.

(b.) This folded side of the Lined Drapery Panel will be placed down to marry to the velcro on the P.M.M. Board*, shown here as on page 233.

(a.) Carefully remove the tape that denotes the middle. Use a disappearing ink pen and mark the middle on the lining side. This ink will start to fade within a few hours, and will completely disappear in 24 hours, so finish the next two steps before the ink is gone.

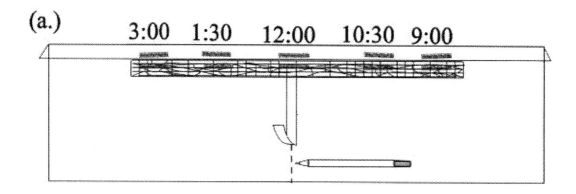

(b.) Fan fold the drapery fabric. Make sure the first fold is turned under, so the drapery fabric shows not the lining fabric. It is really only necessary to make the folds at the center (12:00 o'clock). Make the width of each fold 2".

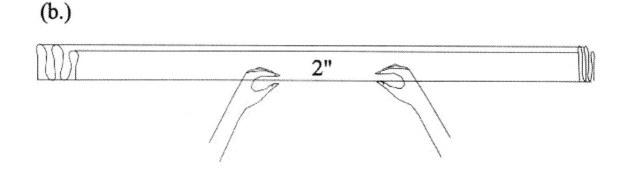

(a.) Place the lining side up so as to work from the underside of the drapery treatment. Leaving the Jute webbing free so it can lay flat on the P.M.M. Board*, pin the folds made at center (12:00 o'clock) with safety pins. Let the rest flow free. If you prefer, a small whipstitch can be made at each fold instead of safety pins.

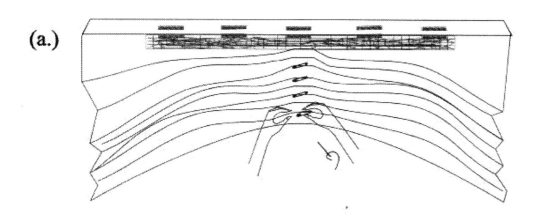

(a.)

(b.) Marry the velcro of the Jute Webbing to the coordinating velcro on the P.M.M. Board*.

(c.) Check for symmetry, readjust as needed.

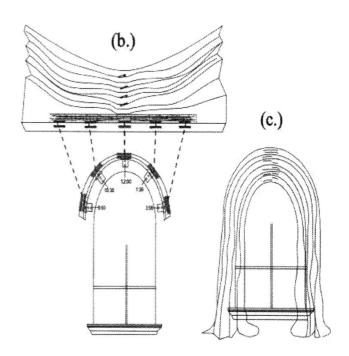

(a.) Slip the skinny tieback where there is small gap between the wall and the P.M.M. Board*. Bring the skinny tie back over the front, catching the folded pleats and tie it underneath the P.M.M.Board*, so it won't be seen.

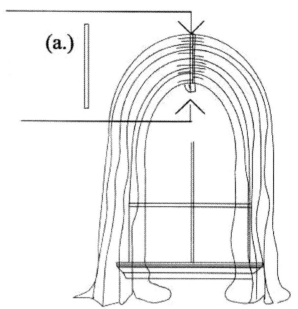

(b.) When finished, the decorative brass tie back will be placed directly under the 12:00 o'clock corner iron, so allow enough slack in the tie back for the folded pleats to come down approximately to this level.

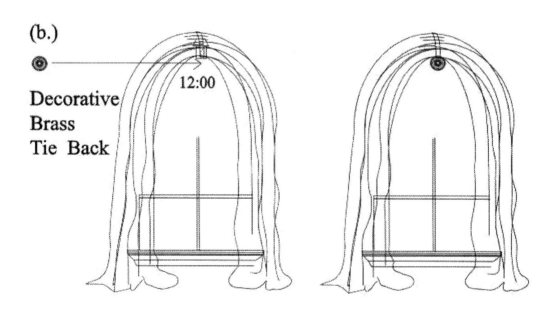

(a.) Slip the skinny tie back in place at the 9:00 o'clock position, where there is a small gap between the wall and the P.M.M. Board*.

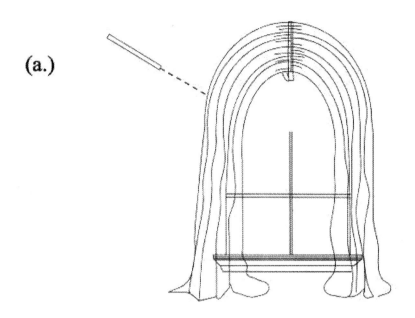

(b.) To make the folds of the swaged Lined Drapery Panel bend your fingers in a "sideways U" shape, so you can use them as a tool to make the pleated folds go in and out.

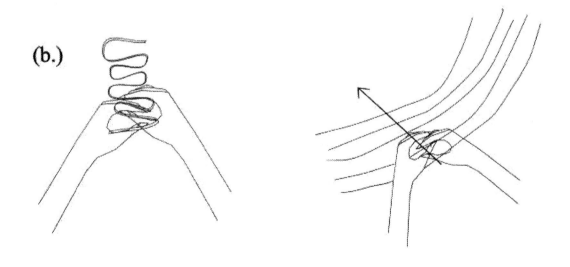

(a.) Make the folds of the Lined Drapery Panel using the "sideways U" as previously shown.

(b.) Start further down past the 9:00 o'clock position on the inside of the panel and angle up as you make the folds, gathering the folds as you go, so you can bring the gathered folds up to the side at the 9:00 o'clock position. Make the folds tighter the closer you get to the P.M.M. Board*. Allow a puff to form in the swag, but keep the folds a little tighter the closer you are to the P.M.M. Board*.

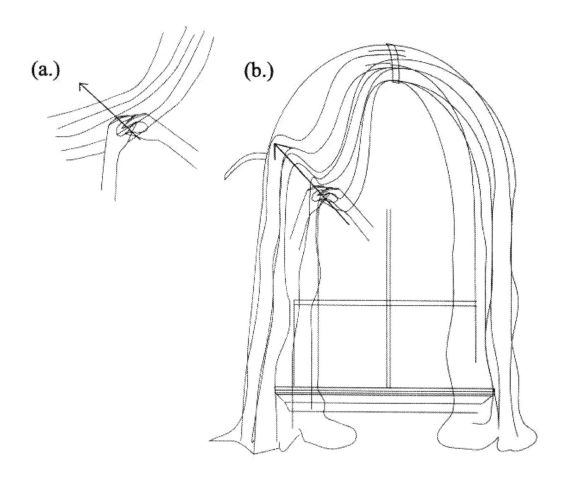

(a.) When satisfied with the swag of the folds, then tie it at the 9:00 o'clock position with the skinny tie back, and knot underneath next to the underside of the P.M.M. Board* so it will not show. Repeat the same for the other side at the 3:00 o'clock position, evaluate for symmetry and readjust as needed.

(b.) Apply the decorative brass tie back so it appears that it is the brass tie backs that are holding back and swaging the drapes, (at 12:00, 3:00, and 9:00 o'clock) instead of the skinny tie backs. Allow the material to puff around the decorative brass tie backs.

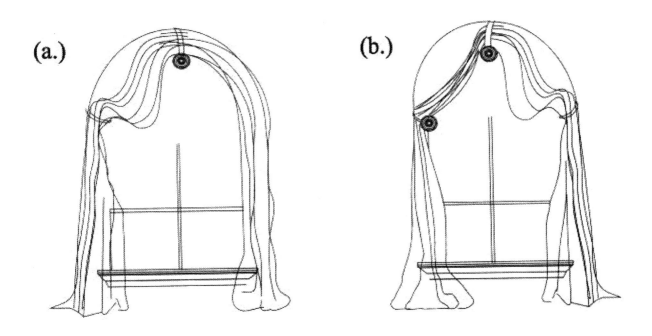

If the P.M.M. Board* does not afford a gap large enough to slip a skinny tie back between the board and the wall, then make the swag folds at the side (3:00 and 9:00 o'clock positions) with safety pins as was done in the 12:00 o'clock position. Use double faced tape to secure the fabric to the brass tie backs.

(a.) If needed, to encourage distinct folds in the drapery panel, fan fold the panel with the "sideways U" bent fingers to make folds go in and out. Wrap scrap pieces of fabric around the folds, to hold them in place. Place them at the top, middle, and bottom of the drapery panel. Allow to stand for 2 to 3 days.

(b.) After removing the scrap pieces of fabric utilized to hold the folds, use a steam iron to remove wrinkles and make the folds smooth. Puddle the excess fabric on the floor. Stand back and evaluate for symmetry and fullness, fluff and puff as needed.

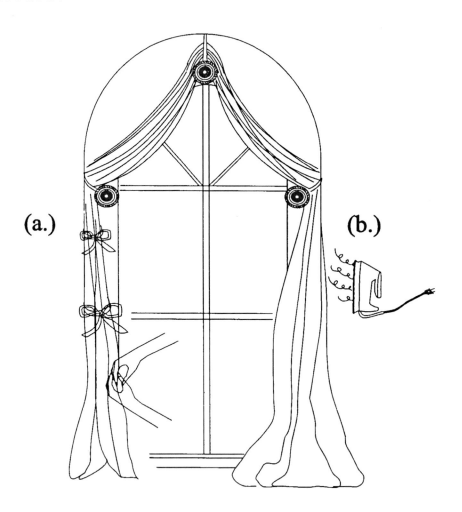

Chapter 11
Proportion Calculations To Make Swags Sizes in Proportion When Window Sizes Vary

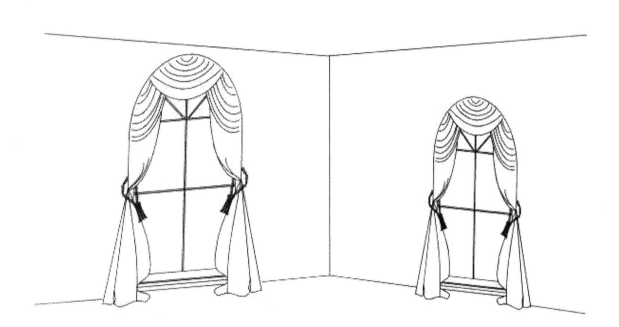

New home designs often have more than one palladian window in a room, or in adjoining rooms that are treated as one big open space. Often these windows will vary in size. To make the swags of each window look proportioned in scale to each other then use a simple proportion calculation equation (named A. O.K.) to figure out the swag size of each window. A calculator will make this a snap, otherwise use long division and multiplication. Details on the following pages.

For example you have a swag pattern that makes a finished swag that is 24" in width across the top, and the plan is to apply the triple swag treatment to an arched window that is 41" in width across the top (where the window is straight, at approximately 3:00 and 9:00 o'clock). You also have a larger arched window that is 56" in width, and if you apply the same triple swag treatment, then the swags will appear much smaller in size by comparison. The answer to make them appear the same in proportion is to make the 56" window's swag bigger. But how much bigger?

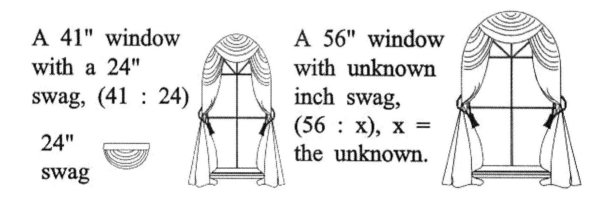

The proportion calculation equation named "A. OK.", a little jingle to help one remember, stands for "Available is to Ordered" (available : 1 = ordered : x), what you have and what you need. What you have is 41" window with a 24" swag, (41 : 24). What you need, is to know how much larger to make the swag for a 56" window, (56 : x). " A. OK." A 41" window is to a 24" swag, as a 56" window is to a (x") swag, the equation is 41 : 24 = 56 : x.

To work this equation, 41 : 24 = 56 : x, first multiply the two inner numbers on each side of the equation and then multiply the two outer numbers on each side of the equation.

$$41 : 24 = 56 : x$$

(2nd: outer pair; 1st: inner pair)

which is: 24 X 56 = 41 X (x)
which is: 1344 = 41(x)

to find out what (x) is, divide both sides of the equation by 41,

1344/41 = 41(x)/41

which is: 32.7 = (x).

Round up to 33 and this is the finished width of the larger swag.

Your enlarged swag's width should be 33" across the top to achieve the same ratio and scale on a 56" wide window as does the 24" wide swag does on a 41" window. There is a 9" difference between the two swags (33 - 24 = 9), so you will need to enlarge your swag pattern by a total of 9".

To enlarge the swag pattern by a total of 9" for example, you will need to work from the folded edge of the swag pattern, so it can be evenly duplicated both sides of the swag. Since you will be working from the folded edge of the swag and new pattern, the fold will essentially double the number, so only 1/2 of this number 9", (4 1/2") will be the working distance from the folded edge.

The easiest way to enlarge a swag pattern is to make your own pattern using the original swag pattern as a guide. The material used for your own pattern can be either muslin, or a grid lined Pellon material found in fabric stores specifically made for enlarging patterns, or brown paper taped together, or brown craft paper, or newspaper.

(a.) Fold the swag pattern in half lengthwise so the cut out zig zag is only on one side.

(b.) Fold your own pattern material in half lengthwise.

(a.) fold swag pattern in half lengthwise

(b.) Fold your own pattern material in half lenghtwise.

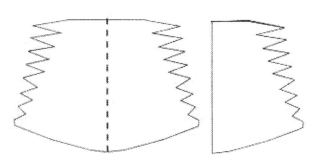

Place the fold of the pattern swag, 1/2 of the (x) number of inches away from the folded edge of your own pattern material. In this case (x) = 9, and 1/2 of (x) = 4 1/2". So the folded swag pattern is placed 4 1/2" away from the folded edge of your own pattern material (muslin, or grid lined Pellon, or brown paper etc.) Make sure the top, middle, and bottom portions of the folded edge of the swag pattern are equal distance from the folded edge of your own pattern material. Also leave enough room at the top and bottom to add 1 /2" to the new pattern.

(a.) Using a sewing gauge, place the folded swag pattern 4 1/2" away from the folded edge of the enlarging material, allow for 1 /2" at the top and bottom.

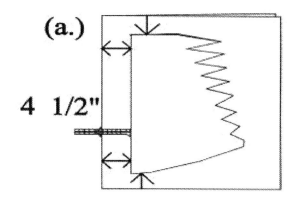

(b.) Pin the folded swag pattern in place, cut out along the sides of the zig zag of the swag pattern, and add 1 /2" at the top and bottom of the swag pattern.

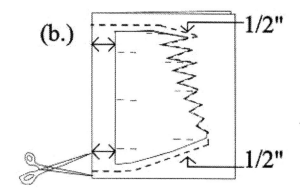

Use your own new swag pattern to make all three swags for the triple swag treatment for the larger window. Before you use this pattern on your expensive drapery material try it out on some inexpensive muslin and pin it together as you would if you were making a finished swag. Make any minor changes as needed to the muslin by folding the swag in half lengthwise, so the change will be even on both sides of the swag. Use the revised muslin as your new swag pattern.

Unless the original swag pattern is made to be specifically cut on the bias (where the material is turned so the weave will run diagonally instead of straight up and down), then fold your own swag pattern lengthwise, so the cut out is on one side, and place it on the fold lengthwise on the drapery material, as you did when making the original swag pattern.

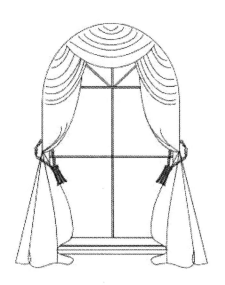
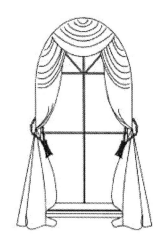

Chapter 12
How To Give A Traditional Square Window A Palladian Arched Look

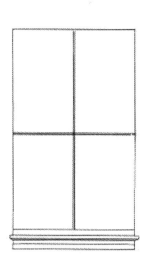 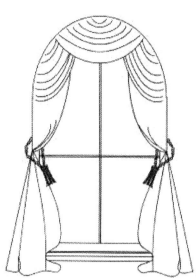

Palladian arches can add architectural interest to a room, now you can achieve a Palladian arched look for square windows by using a few tricks. The secret is to use blackout lining, like the kind used in hotel draperies, and to use a top treatment that will hang down far enough to hide the square shape of the window. The "Outside Mount Triple Swag" and the "Single Swag" applications are suitable for this ploy. These window treatments will allow enough of the curtain to drape down from the half round Palladian arch to ensure hiding the square shape of the window.

* Polystyrene Lattice Strip abbreviated as P.L. Strip*.
* Polystyrene Moulding Mounting Board abbreviated as P.M.M. Board*.

Check List For Tools and Supplies

* Directions and Checklist for Tools and Supplies for chapter 1 "The Outside Mount"
* Directions for chapter 7 " The Outside Mount Triple Swag"
* Or Directions for Chapter 9 " Single Swag"
* Roll of string
* Pencil
* Masking tape
* Black out drapery lining
* Drapery fabric
* Metal tape measure

The blackout lining will prevent sunlight from outlining the square shape of the window as it shines through the curtain during the day. When using the blackout drapery lining place the rubbery side of the lining to the wrong side of the drapery fabric, so the side that shows is not the rubbery side, this will give the window treatment a more polished look.

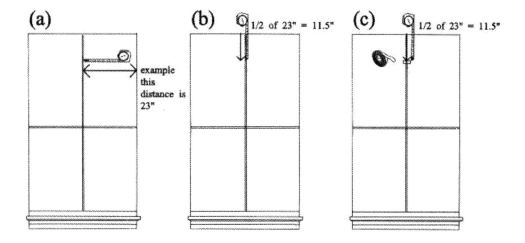

(a) Measure from the side edge of the window to the middle of the window.

(b) Divide this number in half, this is for the measurement needed to come down from the top of the window.

(c) Find the middle of the top of the square window and come down this many inches and mark the window with a piece of masking tape.

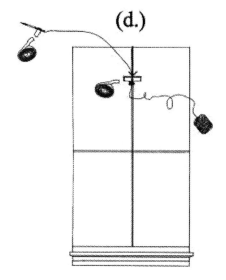

(d) Take a long piece of string, longer than you desire the arch of the window to reach, tie a knot in one end. With the masking tape, tape a pencil to one end of the string, and tape the other end of the string, with the knot, down to the piece of tape already on the window marking the spot. Place the knot under the tape so the string will not slip.

(a.) Decide how far out the arch is to reach, a good rule of thumb is for the arch to clear the top corners of the square by 3". Tape up the string to the pencil for this desired distance, with the other end of the string knotted and secured to the window pane, stretch the string out and lightly mark an arc with the pencil onto the wall around the window with the distance of the string as your guide. Start and stop the arc at the same level as the string that is taped to the window pane. These will be the 3:00 and 9:00 o'clock reference points. Use a measuring tape and a level to ensure the arch is symmetrical. Ensure that the middle of the arch falls at the center of the window, 12:00 o'clock, and that 3:00 and 9:00 o'clock are equal distance from the sides of the window. The 1:30 and 10:30 clock positions are positioned halfway between 3:00 and 12:00, and 9:00 and 12:00 o'clock.

(b.) Follow the directions in chapter 1 "The Outside Mount" using the arc as a guide where to place the corner irons.

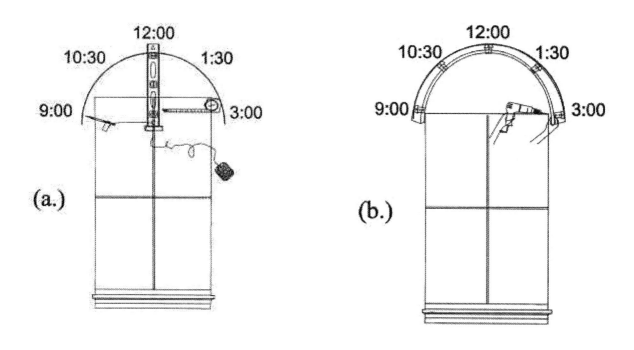

(a.) Be sure the swag treatments will hang down far enough to cover the "squareness" of the window. It will be helpful to make a test swag with muslin to check for the length of the top treatment and hold it up to the arc made before making the holes for the corner irons. Either make the swags larger, or if the arc needs to be made lower. This can be easily achieved by either erasing the previously made penciled arc with an art gum eraser or painting over it.

(a.) As long as most of the middle swag covers most of the top of the square of the window it should be fine, especially if this top treatment is combined with the "Rod Pocket Sleeve With A Diagonal Cut To Fit Arched Windows" as the drapery panel. This panel treatment will help ensure to cover the straight top of the window.

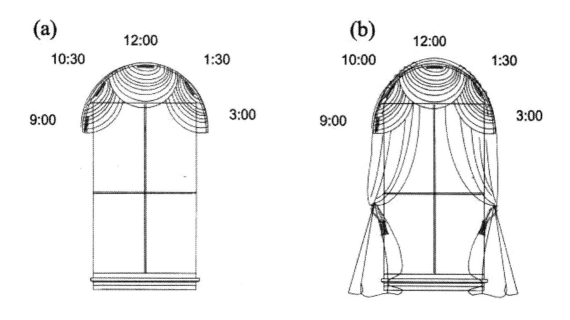

(a.) As mentioned, the best drapery panel application to complete the Palladian look for the traditional window is the "Rod Pocket Sleeve Drapery Panels With A Diagonal Cut To Fit Arched Windows".

(b.) However, the drapery panel application, "Two Short Side Boards Drapery Panels" (chapter 6) is a viable option to use with "Outside Mount Triple Swag", provided the top treatment is long enough to completely cover the square top of the window frame.

Following the directions in chapter 1 "The Outside Mount" to mount the P.M.M. Board* and hardware. Then turn to the desired top window treatment chapter either "Outside Mount Triple Swag" chapter 7 or "Single Swag" chapter 9 and follow the basic directions except substituting the "Black Out" lining for the drapery lining.

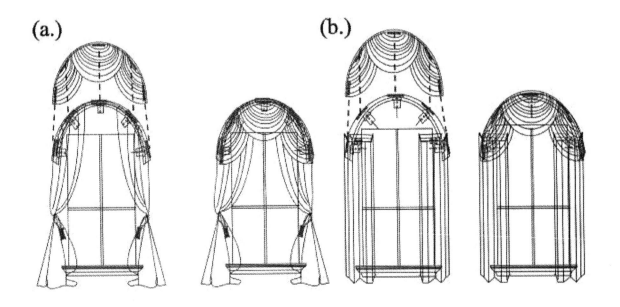

Glossary

Application - The way in which a drapery treatment is attached to the drapery hardware.

Bias - Fabric that is cut so that the direction of the weave runs diagonally rather than horizontally and vertically. When material is cut on the bias so that the weave is diagonal it gives the properties of stretch to the fabric. This is particularly useful when making cording for pillows and makes the folds of swags lay smoother.

Bishop Sleeve - Term use to describe the shape of how a drapery panel is puffed into a tied back fashion to resemble the shape of a Bishop's sleeve.

Bottom hem - The way in which the raw edges of the bottom of a drapery panel are finished, usually turned under 4" to 6" twice.

Clock positions - Term used to describe the positions on the Palladian (half round) arch so to serve as reference points using the clock analogy. The clock positions are 12:00, 1:30, 3:00, 9:00, and 10:30. They are roughly as they appear on the face of a clock. The corner irons that support the P.M.M. Board* of the arched window treatment are placed at each of the clock positions.

Corner Irons - A metal support and attachment device (shaped as an L) that is used with screws to attach two pieces of hard surfaced materials together at right angles. Also sometimes referred to as "angle brackets" and "L brackets". Found in hardware stores.

Crinoline - A stiff light weight band of material used as a drapery header to give body and stiffen the top of drapery panels. Found in fabric stores.

Double Hem - The raw edges of a fabric are finished by turning under twice and stitched to the underside of a garment or drapes.

Drapery Header - Material used to make the top of drapery panels stiff and have body.

Drapery Panel - The portion of a window treatment where the fabric is the full length from the top of the window to the window sill or floor.

Drapery Weighted Fabrics - Fabric material woven to have properties which enhances the ability of the fabric to hang and drape well.

Dye Lot - Refers to the fabric that was dyed in the same batch of dye. Dye batches of the same color may vary slightly from each other.

Half Dimension Swags - A top window treatment involving two swags in which each swag covers one half of the window.

Heat and Bond - An iron on fusible webbing used to join two pieces of fabric together. Found in fabric stores.

Hem - Term used to describe how the raw edges of a fabric are finished, by turning up and stitching to the underside of the garment or drapes.

Inside Mount - The way in which a window treatment's hardware is hung in relationship to the window's frame. The inside mount refers to a window treatment's hardware and drapery treatment being mounted within the inside of the window frame.

Iron on Hem Binding Tape - A fusible colored tape that is used to match the material it is being used for, so a hem can be made without stitching.

Jute Webbing - A coarse woven band of material used in upholstery. Also used in some arched window treatments to provide structural support and a base for the top treatment. Found in fabric stores.

Lining Fabric - A woven material fabric usually white or ivory in color use to be paired with drapery fabric. Lining fabrics add volume and body to the drapery fabric.

Nap - The direction in which the fabric is woven which creates a sheen quality in the fabric that denotes whether the fabric is right side up or upside down.

No Sew - Term used to describe the adjoining of objects or fabrics without the use of needles and thread. Most often a fusible webbing, hot glue, fabric glue, thumbtacks, and or staples are used to bind the materials together.

Outside Mount - The way in which a window treatment's hardware is hung in relationship to the window frame, mounted outside of the window frame.

Palladian - A term used to describe the architectural half round shape of an arch or window design.

Polystyrene Lattice Strip - A flexible thin long strip of polystyrene moulding. It is used to be mounted on top of the Polystyrene Moulding Mounting Board, to provide the flexibility needed to work with drapery fabric. It is secured to the Polystyrene Moulding Mounting Board with velcro. Found in hardware stores.

Polystyrene Moulding Mounting Board - A semiflexible moulding board made of polystyrene, can be used to conform to the shape of an arched window. As an outside mount it is held in place with corner irons. Often it is used in combination with the Polystyrene Lattice Strip. Found in hardware stores.

Repeat - Refers to where the print or design of a fabric starts and stops. Repeat information is helpful when making drapes or decor in that the print can be centered or start and stop in the same place, so objects of decor will appear even and symmetrical. Often the repeat information can be found in the selvage edge.

Right side of fabric - The side of the fabric with print or a decorative raised weave showing.

Rod Pocket sleeve - The way in which fabric is sewn so as to create a sleeve or pocket in the top of a drapery panel so the panel can be gathered on a rod.

Selvage Edge - The edges in the width of a fabric where the manufacture has finished the edges, Often in printed fabrics the color of the print has stopped at the selvage edge and the selvage edge is white with information detailing where the repeat of the fabric starts and stops, as well as the colors used in the print. In solid colored fabrics often the color extends to the selvage edge with the only noticeable difference is a slight change in the weave of the fabric. Fabric tends to rip evenly from selvage edge to selvage edge rather than tearing evenly along the length of the fabric.

Sheers - A window treatment made of a light weight semi see through fabric used to place over a window to diffuse sunlight and allow for some privacy. Commonly sheers are used under drapery panels for an added sense of traditional formality.

Short Side Boards - Term used to describe an attachment device for drapery panels of the Palladian window treatment. The short side boards which drapery panels are fastened to are placed on both sides of a Palladian window to give the illusion of the window treatment being of all one piece. Short side boards are used in combination with a top drapery treatment to help create the illusion of a one piece window treatment.

Side Hem - The way in which the side raw edges of a drapery panel are finished. Usually the raw edges are turned under 1 " to 1 1 /2" twice and stitched to the lining or wrong side of the fabric.

Single Swag - A top window treatment involving only one swag which is positioned in the center at the top of the window, and placed under drapery panels.

Stationary Window Treatment - A non-moving window treatment that is stationary, it is used for decorative purposes only with no operating function to open or close.

Swags - A top drapery treatment in which the fabric material is draped into folds that form a semi-circular shape and placed across the top of a window.

Tie Backs - Item used to hold back drapery panels to the side of a window frame, so the glass of the window remains open to the view. Tie backs are commonly made of drapery fabric and a stiffening inner fabric either buckram, crinoline or such. Also decorative ready made tie backs holders made of decorative ropes and tassels are available.

Top Drapery Treatment - Refers to the drapery treatment that is placed at the top of the window frame. The top treatment can be used alone or can be used in combination with an under drapery treatment.

Triple Swags - A top window treatment involving three swags in which each swag over laps and covers approximately 1/3 of the top of the window.

Under Drapery Treatment - Refers to the drapery panel treatment which is placed under a top drapery treatment.

Wrong Side of Fabric - The side of the fabric without a print or decorative features, not meant to be shown.

About the Author

About the author, Diane has come from a long line of seamstresses who have sewn to enhance the lives of their families and their homes. Her grandmother was a professional seamstress. Her mother had sewn her children's clothes till they were teenagers. As teenagers they begged for store-bought clothes only to come back when they were grown and beg mom to sew the beautiful wedding gowns and bridesmaid dresses that they wore on their special day. Nowadays granddaughter begs for "Mimi" to make her prom dresses.

Diane has not had much experience with sewing garments, but she has excelled in sewing drapes and decor for the home. She developed the idea for the arched window treatment for the do-it-yourselfer and with encouragement from family and friends went on to patent the idea. Now she has written this book so the "Arched Window Solution" can be affordable to everyone.